Priest and People

Priest and People

by Joseph H. Fichter

Loyola University of the South

Sheed and Ward: New York

Contents

Clergy-Lay Relations

The survey of relations between priests and parishioners is a natural outcome of the sociological research that we began more than fifteen years ago in the study of a Southern Catholic parish. This was followed by an analysis of lay societies in a German parish, and by a year-long study of a parochial school in the Midwest. In these and similar research projects we found always that the religious professionals are the key persons in the operation of the Catholic Church, and we subsequently gathered materials for an analysis of religion as an occupation.[1]

While the Catholic laity is active everywhere in support of the clergy, the functioning relationship between the two—between parishioner and priest—tends to be de-emphasized by any separate study of either clergy or laity. The present book is an attempt to supply this need—to analyze the manner in which priests and people relate to each other, and how they differ in their mutual estimation. It is based on the reports of 2,183 diocesan parish priests, and of 2,216 adult Catholics who are their best parishioners.

Obviously, this is only one example of the multiple clerical-lay relationships that exist in the American Catholic Church.

We have focused on the diocesan parish priest because of the lack of research data that would allow other kinds of analysis.[2] We cannot compare the professional clergy across denominational lines. It is beyond our present scope to attempt a comparison of the Catholic priest with the Protestant minister or the Jewish rabbi. Any of these clergymen could again be compared in national or ethnic sub-categories, like the Irish, or German, or Spanish priests.[3] Still further differences are found within the Catholic clergy among contemplative monks, religious order priests, and the diocesan clergy.

Even when we have concentrated only on the diocesan clergy, we find these men actively engaged in a variety of professional roles. Most of the diocesan priests are assigned to parishes, but others have specialized roles as college professors or school teachers, diocesan administrators, editors, scientists. For purposes of analytical refinement and control, therefore, the present discussion deals only with diocesan priests who are in full-time parish work.

In 1959, the diocesan clergy numbered 31,961, and five years later, in 1964, they had increased to 35,077. The parish priests among them constitute the single largest category of priests in the United States, and they are closely associated with more Catholic lay people than any other type of priest. By an interval sample from the *Catholic Directory*, we contacted every seventh diocesan priest actively engaged in parish work. Excluding Hawaii and Alaska, we received from these 4,560 priests 47 percent responses. A similar high proportion of lay parishioners responded, and their regional distribution is shown in Table 1.[4]

The average age of these priests is 41.3 years, with one-fifth of them (21%) being over fifty years of age, and about the same proportion (19%) under thirty. On the average they

TABLE 1—Regional distribution of diocesan priests, as compared to parish priests and laity responding to this study.

| | | *Responses from:* | |
	All Diocesan Priests	*Diocesan Parish Priests*	*Parish Laity*
New England	13%	12%	13%
The East	27	24	22
South Atlantic	4	4	5
Midwest	24	27	26
South Central	3	3	3
Great Plains	13	15	14
Southwest	5	5	6
The West	3	3	4
Pacific Coast	7	6	7

have been priests for almost fifteen years (14.9 years). Three out of ten (29%) have been ordained more than twenty years, and one-fourth of them have been priests for five years or less. Nine out of ten were born in the United States, the principal source of immigrant priests being Ireland, Canada, and Italy.[5] More than eight out of ten (83%) made their theological studies in this country, and about half of these attended the major seminary in their own diocese.

These diocesan priests have experienced the range of activities that may be expected among parish priests in the United States. The great majority (79%) have had full-time assignments in more than one parish, and one-fifth of them have served in five or more different parishes. A substantial minority (27%) had other full-time Church work before going into the parish, the most frequent of which was teaching and military chaplaincies. About one-fifth (19%) of them had started out in other careers even before entering the seminary. Four out of ten came from families that had below-average income when they were in their teens.

The parishioners, like the priests, represent proportionately every diocese in the continental United States, but they are not a representative cross-section of the total American Catholic laity.[6] These are the friends of parish priests. We sought answers only from adult, active, faithful Catholics, who were recommended by their priests as nuclear or modal parishioners. We have, therefore, information only from those who cooperate most with the priests, and may be presumed to know most about the clergy.[7]

These lay people average 41.9 years of age, practically the same average age of the priests. Only one out of ten (11%) is below thirty years of age, and one-fifth (21%) of them are over fifty years of age. Despite the fact that women are commonly more active than men in Church affairs, the larger proportion of these lay people (58%) are males. Since all of these people are twenty-five years of age and older, only a small proportion (15%) are single; eight out of ten (81%) are married, and the small remainder are widowed or separated. Thirty-five percent are college graduates, and one-fifth more attended college. At the other end of the educational range, one-seventh (14%) did not attend, or did not finish, high school.

Like the priests they are here appraising, these active lay parishioners live all over the United States, from the smallest village to the largest metropolis. About one-fifth (18%) live in rural areas with less than 2,500 population, and one-fourth (26%) live in cities with over 100,000 population. They are employed in a large range of occupations and professions. Their five most-mentioned occupations are, in order of frequency: salesman, office worker, teacher, skilled worker, and engineer. The great majority are from middle-income families; but more than one-fourth (27%) say that their income is above average, and less than one out of ten (8%) that it is below average.

The collection of data on this study was done in two waves, starting with the priests. Fifty days after the first mailing, we sent out a postcard reminder to all of the priests in the sample since we had no way, or intention, of identifying those who had returned the completed questionnaire. We had promised a brief report of the general findings to every priest who sent in his name and address separately. More than 1,500 priests asked for this report. When we sent it to them we included three questionnaires to be distributed to the most active and cooperative adult Catholics in different parishes operated by diocesan priests.

These materials were coded and the data punched on IBM cards in the Sociology Research Workshop of Loyola University, and were then transposed to electronic tapes at the Computer Center of Tulane University. Dr. James Sweeney, professor and director of the Computer Center, gave invaluable counsel and cooperation throughout the processing of data. To him, and his assistants, William Nettleton and Daniel Kileen, are due much of the exactness and clarity of this research report.

Financial support for this project came from three sources. Besides the general research support from Loyola University of the South on all phases of the study, most of the expense of the priest survey was carried by a grant from the American Philosophical Society, and for the laity study by a grant from the Social Science Research Council. Without this kind of generous assistance from these foundations, most research of this type could not be carried on.

One of the fruitful techniques of interpretation used in this study was the group interview with diocesan priests and with lay parishioners. When certain generalizations began to emerge from the raw data, we sought explanations and interpretations from these people. For this purpose we visited twenty-two cities in various parts of the country. We held group interviews with parish clergy only in Atlanta, Detroit, and Pittsburg, and with parishioners only in Buffalo, Newark, and Seattle. We interviewed separate groups of priests and laity in the other cities: Boston, Chicago, Cincinnati, Dallas, Denver, Los Angeles, Milwaukee, New Orleans, New York, Oklahoma City, Portland, St. Louis, St. Paul, San Francisco, Scranton, and South Bend.

What is said in this book, then, is the report of the diocesan parish priests and their people, given first in questionnaires, and then explained in these group interviews. Their cooperation, anonymous as it remains, is duly acknowledged and fully appreciated here. In processing and classifying the data, much of the monotonous, routine labor was performed by Diane Griffin, Leah Jacob, and Rhoda Viellion. The final version of the manuscript was typed by Carmen Kelly.

To all of these persons, named and unnamed, to the research foundations and university administrators, goes the credit for whatever basic value a study of this kind has. The research design, formulation and testing of hypotheses, and presentation of materials are the responsibility of the author.

NOTES

1. For the main publications on this sequence of research projects, see the following books by Joseph H. Fichter, *Southern Parish: Dynamics of a City Church* (Chicago: University of Chicago Press,

1951), *Social Relations in the Urban Parish* (Chicago: University of Chicago Press, 1954), *Soziologie der Pfarrgruppen* (Muenster: Aschendorff Verlag, 1957), *Parochial School: A Sociological Study* (Notre Dame: University of Notre Dame Press, 1958), and *Religion as an Occupation: A Study in the Sociology of Professions* (Notre Dame: University of Notre Dame Press, 1961).

2. David O. Moberg, *The Church as a Social Institution* (Englewood Cliffs: Prentice-Hall, 1962), ch. 18, "The Clergy," and W. Seward Salisbury, *Religion in American Culture* (Homewood: Dorsey Press, 1964), ch. 10, "The Clergy," bring together most of the available comparative references. For an empirical study with comparative pertinence, see W. Widick Schroeder, "Lay Expectations of the Ministerial Role: An Exploration of Protestant-Catholic Differentials," *Journal for the Scientific Study of Religion,* vol. 2, no. 2 (Spring, 1963), pp. 217-227.

3. We were able to make comparisons between native and foreign-born, and between Latin and Anglo-Saxon priests, in a research project reported in *Cambio Social En Chile* (Santiago de Chile: Editorial Universidad Catolica, 1962), ch. 4, "Clero Nacional y Extranjero."

4. The regional divisions used here are the same as those employed by the United States Bureau of the Census, and by the compilers of the *Official Catholic Directory* (New York: Kenedy). The descriptive terminology has been changed.

5. Only 6 percent of the young priests, under thirty years of age, are foreign-born, as compared to 20 percent of the priests who are over sixty years old.

6. This distinction must be remembered throughout. The clergy in this study are a scientific, representative cross-section of American diocesan parish priests. The lay respondents are the "better" Catholics who live in parishes directed by diocesan priests. Therefore, valid comparisons cannot be made with studies in which the total parish population is represented.

7. For the criteria employed to categorize nuclear, modal, marginal, and dormant parishioners, see Fichter, *Social Relations in the Urban Parish,* pp. 7-79. The fact that some modal parishioners are also active members and close friends of the priest was further recog-

nized by Frank Cizon, "Some Characteristics of Lay Leaders in a
Catholic Suburban Parish," paper read at the meeting of the Religious Research Association (Indianapolis, June 16, 1961). For a
Protestant analogy, see Martin E. Marty, "The Remnant: Retreat
and Renewal," *Christian Century,* vol. 75 (November 26, 1958),
pp. 1361-1365.

Priest and People

CHAPTER ONE

The Closest Friends

The parish priest is ideally all things to all men, but he is separated by ordination and function from the laity. His pastoral and fatherly role is focused directly on his own parishioners, but his missionary role reaches out to all souls, regardless of their religious and denominational affiliation.[1] By the sheer fact of living and working in a community, however, the parish priest has more frequent contact with some people than with others. Like every other human being he is drawn closer to some individuals than to others. To what extent he would call this a bond of personal friendship may be left in doubt since about one out of ten of our priest respondents says that he has no "best friend" among the laity.

The large number of lay persons (2,216) who provided information for this study were recommended by their priests as exemplary, cooperative parishioners. They are presumably recognized by both clergy and laity for their active interest in the Church and its works, and for this reason they may be expected to have more than a passing acquaintance with the parish clergy.[2] From this point of view, all of them may well be called friends of the priest.

Obviously, the clerical-lay relationship can be classified in many ways. In this instance we sought to derive two categories of parishioners: those who are close friends and those who are distant friends of the priest. The norm of classification was the frequency with which these people had priest visitors in their home. One-third of them said that the parish priest had not been in their home at all during the past year, and forty-five percent said no other priest had visited them. On the other hand, almost one out of five said the parish priest visited them often, and almost one out of seven said the same about the non-parish priests.

TABLE 1—Comparative frequency of visits to parishioners by parish and non-parish priests.

	Parish Priests	Non-parish Priests
Not at all	33%	45%
Only once	18	12
Several times	30	29
Often	19	14

By combining these statistics we are able to make a clear-cut distinction between the "closest" and the "distant" lay friends of the clergy. Those who said they had been visited "often" during the past year by either the parish priest or some other priest, or by both, we have categorized as the closest friends of the clergy. Those who said there was no priest at all in their home during the past year, we have termed the distant friends of the clergy. Although this appears to be a logical method of designating the degree of friendship, a note of caution must be injected here. Some priests do not, on principle, visit the homes of their parishioners, except on sick calls and in emergencies.[3] Some lay people prefer to visit the parish rectory and may thus develop a close friendship with clergymen who never come to their homes.[4]

In the present discussion we are interested in learning something about these friends since they are the type of parishioner likely to have the clearest image of the priest. The significant factor is, of course, clerical friendship, and in order to isolate this factor we match the two categories for sex and age. In each group six out of ten (61%) are males, and the rest females. The average age for both close and distant friends is 42.2 years, with one-fourth of them below thirty-five years of age, and one-fourth fifty years or older. Since priests tend to visit families rather than individuals, we eliminated the unmarried respondents from both categories. Though not numerous, mixed marriages are twice as likely (9%) among the distant than among the close (5%) friends of priests. On the other hand, converts to Catholicism are more likely than non-converts to be visited frequently by the parish priests.

TABLE 2—Comparative frequency of parish priests' visits to the homes of converts and non-converts.

	(272)	(1944)
	Converts	Non-converts
Not at all	25%	35%
Only once	17	18
Several times	35	29
Often	23	18

The obvious assumption we are making in this comparison is that the closest friends of priests have a more perceptive knowledge of the clergyman than do the distant friends. We should like to know too what kinds of people priests choose

for their best friends, and what perceptible effect the friendship of a priest may have on the laity. Our data allow us to test
several related sub-hypotheses: (a) Are the closest friends
most sympathetic to the work of the priest? (b) Are they more
appreciative of the priesthood in general? (c) Are they more
progressive in their social attitudes and awareness? (d) Are
they better educated than the distant friends? (e) Are they of
a higher social class?

Sympathetic Friends

The first hypothesis that we will examine here is the assumption that the closest friends of the priest have the most sympathetic attitude toward his burden of work. Parishioners seem
generally agreed that the priest works hard, but they are often
vague about what the priest does with his time. One of our
respondents, a junior executive, feels that this is not unique.
"Often," he says, "you don't know what work your own associates are doing. You see a man striding around the office with
papers under his arm and you assume that he is terribly busy."
Nevertheless, since close friends are presumed to know more
about the parish priest, they may be expected to have a clearer
understanding of his parochial work.

TABLE 3—Comparative percentage responses of close and distant
friends on priests' three most time-consuming tasks.

	(275) Closest	(275) Distant
Financial administration	31%	42%
Counselling	20	11
Directing organizations	11	11

The two categories of friends give the same rank order of
time-consuming tasks, but the distant friends emphasize more

the administrative role of the priest, while the closest friends recognize more the role of counselling. Among other parochial activities the close friends emphasize the work of convert instruction, while the distant friends see the priest more often in the confessional. It must be pointed out that more (60%) of the distant than of the close friends (48%) say that they are better acquainted with a pastor than with a curate. It is a fact that pastors have greater financial responsibilities than curates, but there may also be an implication here that curates visit the homes of parishioners more often than pastors do.[5]

While hardly anyone in either group ranks preaching as one of the time-consuming tasks of the priest, both are in agreement in the same proportions (82%) that the sermons they have heard during the past year seem to be well prepared. We then asked them to look at the total job demands made on priests and compare them with the demands made on other professional men, like lawyers, physicians, and engineers. The closest friends are more likely (45%) than the distant friends (36%) to say that the work burdens on the priest are greater than those on other professional men.

TABLE 4—Comparative opinions of the work demands made on priests and on other professional men.

	Closest	Distant
Priest must work harder	45%	36%
About the same	36	41
Not so hard	19	23

In spite of this difference of interpretation concerning the work burdens of the parish priest, the close friends are much more likely (49%) than the distant friends (37%) to say that the priest they know gets his work done efficiently and without too much difficulty. It may be this interpretation of the work habits of the priest that prompts the different responses to the question whether parish priests should have regular office hours. Most parish priests (63%) are themselves opposed to the maintenance of office hours in the rectory; and they have probably expressed this feeling to their friends.[6] At any rate, the closest friends are less in favor (42%) of this formalized arrangement than are the distant friends (50%).

TABLE 5—Comparative opinions concerning the advisability of office hours for the parish priest.

	Closest	Distant
In favor	42%	50%
Neutral	27	23
Opposed	31	27

While all these lay people generally show favorable attitudes toward the hard-working parish priest, the expected tendency of greater sympathy is indicated on the part of the closest friends of priests. The evidence tests out, at least tentatively, in a positive direction for the first hypothesis.

View of Priestly Vocation

The second hypothesis we may form from these data is the assumption that the closest friends of the clergy have a more appreciative view of the priesthood as a vocation. A somewhat higher proportion of the close friends (73%) than of the distant friends (64%) says that the priest they know best is a happy and cheerful person. If a pleasing personality is the best advertisement for the Church vocation, we may expect that these cheerful priests have an influence upon their lay friends' attitudes.

One of the ways of measuring appreciation for the priestly vocation is to study people's attitudes toward the seminary. We put to these parishioners the question: "Suppose you had a son just graduating from elementary school (age 13 years) who feels that he has a vocation to the priesthood. What would you advise him to do?" Almost four out of ten of both categories (39% close friends, 37% distant friends) said that they would advise the boy to enter the minor seminary immediately. Most of the rest would advise him to attend a regular Catholic high school; and a small percentage, about one out of twenty, would want him to attend college before entering the seminary.

Perhaps a more significant insight into the meaning of the seminary vocation is found in answer to the question what a high school senior, who feels that he has a vocation to the priesthood, should do about dating and parties.[7] Here we find a clear difference of opinion between these two categories of respondents. Well over half (56%) of the close friends, as compared to only four out of ten of the others, believe that the young man should either eliminate or decrease these social activities. The distant friends of priests are much more likely

TABLE 6—Comparative opinions about dating and parties for a high school senior with a potential vocation.

| | Parishioners | | (2183) |
	Closest	Distant	Priests
Discontinue or limit dating and parties	30%	23%	38%
Discontinue dating but continue parties	26	17	36
Do as other Catholic boys his age do	41	56	23
Other advice	3	4	3

to say that he should continue to behave like other Catholic
boys his age.

The close friends of the clergy tend more nearly to share
the priests' own opinions concerning the social life of the
prospective seminarian. It is probable that the priests' influence is at work here on their friends. When we asked the laity
to what extent the priest they know best encourages boys to
enter the seminary, a larger proportion (72%) of the closest
friends than of the distant friends (63%) says that the clergy
they know does "very much" or "quite a bit." Thus, it appears
that both the priests and their close friends have a more than
ordinary degree of interest in promoting vocations to the
priesthood.

The evidence is relatively slim in this study, and the conclusion to this hypothesis probably cannot rest alone on these
data. We have seen that all of these parishioners were chosen
by their priests as better-than-average Catholics, and we must
remember that the difference between these two categories of
lay persons would not be so great as that between nuclear
and dormant parishioners. Nevertheless, there is a persuasive
likelihood that the closest friends of the clergy have the more
realistic understanding of the Church vocation.

Socially Alert Laymen

Are the closest friends of priests more progressive and alert
in their social attitudes? The logical expectation in this question may be the supposition that people who have a deep
interest in the Church and its functionaries are also greatly
concerned about the whole society in which they live. Certain
test questions provide little more than hints leading to this
assumption. For example, the closest friends of priests are

only somewhat more likely (54%) than the distant friends (48%) to favor Democratic candidates in the national elections. They are also slightly more in favor (61%) of expanding or maintaining America's foreign economic aid program than are the distant friends (57%) of priests.[8]

These two categories of respondents are quite similar in the way they rank the importance of the major social issues of the United States. They both feel that the reduction of crime and delinquency is of first importance, that the securing of basic civic rights for all Americans regardless of race or creed is second, and that reducing the tensions of the cold war is third. They also agree that the two greatest problems facing the Church in America are Communism and the lack of vocations to the seminary and the religious life.[9]

TABLE 7—Comparative extent to which respondents have increased or maintained interest in selected social issues.

	Closest	Distant
Religious issues	98%	92%
International affairs	94	90
Race relations	86	83
Management–Labor relations	78	72
Community organization	74	61
Music, art, theater	61	54

When we asked these parishioners to what extent they are interested and involved in various social issues of the day, we found that the closest friends of the priests were consistently more socially aware. While in some of these items the statistical differences are not great, there is not one of them in which the distant friends of the priest show as much interest as do the close friends. The cumulation of all of them lends weight to the hypothesis that the close friends are more socially alert and progressive than the others. Since they talk with the priest more often, it is not unexpected that they take more interest in religious matters. Perhaps not so expected is the fact that they also have greater interest in music, art, and the theater.

In so far as we can draw any conclusion from these data, we have perhaps more persuasive than convincing evidence that the closest friends of priests tend toward a liberal social orientation. The tendency is consistent but the explanation for this tendency is somewhat elusive. Probably the priests themselves are slightly less progressive than their closest friends, and it may be that these social attitudes in laymen are due less to clerical influence than to other factors. Elsewhere it has been argued, and demonstrated, that liberal Catholics are more favorable to the clergy (and therefore, less likely to be anti-clerical) than are the conservative Catholics.[10]

Educated Friends

Do the close friends of priests have more education than the distant friends? The assumption may generally be made that people tend to associate more with those who have had schooling similar in extent, if not in kind, to their own. The pastoral function of the priesthood is directed, of course, to all of the parishioners. Thus the priesthood is by intent and function different from any other profession, and one may not so easily assume that the priest is attracted to the more bookish, more learned people, among the active Catholic parishioners.

There is a remarkable similarity in the academic background and experience of these two categories of respondents. Approximately nine out of ten of both are from families in which the parents did not attend college. Almost one out of five (18%) of both close friends and distant friends either did not attend or did not finish high school. About four out of ten of both attended or finished a Catholic high school, and the remaining larger percentages of both finished at a public high school.

TABLE 8—Comparative college education of lay respondents.

	Closest	Distant
Did not attend college	50%	53%
College not completed	21	18
College graduate	29	29

While the close and distant friends of the clergy are quite similar in the amount of their formal educational experience, we may make an estimate of their academic achievement on the basis of the amount and kind of reading they do. In their own self-appraisal, however, seven out of ten of both categories say that they are interested in reading for relaxation, and more than nine out of ten of both claim that they read also for information.

The quality of periodical reading is probably as significant as the amount of reading that people do. Both kinds of respondents read *Life* magazine in about the same proportions (88%); but a larger proportion of the distant friends of priests than of their close friends read the *Saturday Evening Post* and the *Reader's Digest*. All of the more serious periodicals on our check-list, *Atlantic Monthly, Commonweal, America, Time, U. S. News & World Report,* are read by a larger proportion of the closest friends of the clergy.

Here again, we cannot say that the evidence provides a
definite conclusion to the hypothesis that parish priests prefer
to visit the homes of more educated members of their flock.
The parishioners who answered this study are the more active
Catholics, and they undoubtedly have a higher level of schooling than the general population of American Catholics.[11] They
also undoubtedly read more than does the average Catholic.
In the comparisons we have here made, the clergy's closest
friends read the more serious and informative periodicals, but
this evidence does not seem sufficient to allow the conclusion
that they are more educated than the less intimate friends of
the priest. Some factors seem to balance out others. We shall
see, for instance, that priests in small towns know their parishioners rather well. On the other hand, parishioners who attended Catholic schools know their priests rather well, but these
usually live in larger towns and cities where the schools are
located.

Middle-Class Friends

Are the parishioners with whom the priests associate of a
higher social class than other Catholics? There is no question
that the total number of respondents to this study already
represent higher occupational status than the general Catholic
population. Three out of ten (31%) are professional people,
while their proportion is probably less than 10 percent for
American Catholics as a whole. This implies also more years
of education among our respondents, 35 percent of whom
finished college, as compared to an estimated 15 percent
of the Catholic population.

In the present study information is available from both
priests and laity concerning the occupations of Catholics who

are the friends of priests, and who are for the most part nuclear parishioners. In other words, the priests have indicated the occupation of the best friend they have among the laity, and the parishioners have given their own occupation.[12]

TABLE 9—Principal occupations of parishioners, as reported by priests and laity (compared with national sample).

	(1893) Priests	(2210) Laity	(4103) Both	National Sample
Professional	35%	27%	31%	8%
Business and management	16	14	15	11
Clerical and sales	20	30	26	10
Skilled and semi-skilled	12	14	13	42
Service and unskilled	8	5	6	10
Farming	6	4	5	4
Others	3	5	4	15

The parish priests place the highest proportion of their best friends in the professional category, while the largest single category of parishioners who answered this study is made up of clerical and sales workers. In regard to particular occupations, the three mentioned most frequently by the priests are: physicians, teachers, and salesmen. Most frequently mentioned by the laity as their own occupations are, in this order, salesmen, office workers, and teachers. It may be noted in passing that we did not request the priests to distribute the questionnaires to their best friends, but to their best parishioners; and it may be quite likely in many instances that the two terms do not coincide.

Now, in order to compare the closest friends with the distant friends, we are able to use only the responses of the laity. This information demonstrates two significant facts. The first is that there are many more businessmen in the homes the priest

TABLE 10—Comparative occupational categories as reported by closest and distant friends of the clergy.

	(275)	(275)	(2210)
	Closest	*Distant*	*All Laity*
Professional	28%	25%	27%
Business and management	27	11	14
Clerical and sales	22	34	30
Skilled and semi-skilled	14	16	14
Service and unskilled	1	4	5
Farming	3	4	4
Others	5	6	5

visits, and the second is that there are many more clerical and sales workers in the homes he does not visit. In the responses from all of the laity in this study, the large number of office workers swells the occupational category of clerical and sales to a size larger than that of the professionals. Yet the parish priest visits the homes of professional people in considerably greater proportions than he does those of clerical workers.[13]

Besides education and occupation, one of the common criteria for the measurement of social class is that of income. Most of the laity place themselves in the middle income group, and it is these people that the parish priest visits most. Yet the occupational status of the priests' closest friends has given us the hint that their economic status would be over-represented in the above-average income group. While not all of the priests' visits to the homes of parishioners were social calls, it is probably true that parishioners in the higher income brackets are in a better position to entertain visitors in their homes. These are the people who are more likely than others to extend invitations to their friends, including the clergy.

The general assumption that the closest friends of the clergy are of a higher economic class than are the distant friends

TABLE 11—Comparative economic status of priests' friends as indicated by reported income.

	(275)	(275)	(2216)
	Closest	*Distant*	*All Laity*
Above average	31%	24%	27%
Middle income	63	66	65
Below average	6	10	8

tends to be verified by the way these two categories of respondents compare their own material standard of living with that of the priest they know best. The closest friends are much more (27%) likely than the distant (17%) to say that their own standard of living is higher than that of the clergy. In spite of their advantaged economic position, however, they are also more likely (66%) than the distant friends (57%) to say that their own financial worries are greater than those of the priest they know best.

TABLE 12—Comparison of laity's standard of living with that of priest friend.

	(275)	(275)	(2216)
	Closest	*Distant*	*All Laity*
Laity's is higher	27%	17%	22%
About the same	56	53	54
Laity's is lower	17	29	23

This hypothesis about the class status of the clergy's closest friends is clearly proved out by the data of this study. The respondents for the most part are of the middle class. While the parish priest has been in two-thirds of the homes of these respondents in the past year, and while the greatest percentage of his visits are to middle-class families, his closest friends are of higher social status than his distant friends.

Summary

This analysis provides a fairly clear picture of the kinds of parishioners with whom the priest associates most frequently. We have controlled carefully the factors of age, sex, and marital status in matching the close and distant friends. Thus, the principal factor of clerical friendship has been isolated, but we must avoid the unwarranted assumption that these parishioners act and think the way they do *because* they are friends of priests. We may readily assume that they are in some ways influenced by the friendship of a priest, but that there are obviously also many other influences working upon them.

By controlling our matching samples for age, sex, and marital status, we were able to ascertain the various characteristics of laymen closely associated with the clergy. The closest friends of priests—those whose homes are visited most by the clergy—are more likely to be converts, and less likely to be in mixed marriages, than is the case with the distant friends of priests. On the assumption that these lay people are fairly well acquainted with the parish priests, we may outline several aspects of our findings.

1. The closest friends of the clergy seem to have a more sympathetic understanding of the parish priest, a greater appreciation of his role, and a better knowledge of his work.

2. Their general attitude toward the priestly vocation and the expectations of seminary training is also one of sympathetic appreciation. They probably have also a greater interest in promoting vocations to the seminary.

3. From the point of view of progressive social orientation, there appears to be little difference between the closest and distant friends of priests, except that the closest friends show consistently more interest in social issues.

4. There is no significant difference in the educational attainments of these two categories of parishioners, although it must be remembered that this whole study embraces a higher percentage of college graduates than the Catholic population.
5. The fact that professional and business men are more numerous among the closest friends of priests may imply that they have more education. They are also somewhat more likely to be in the upper income brackets, although priests visit mostly the families of the middle class.

NOTES

1. Using mainly French materials, Paul Furfey, "The Missionary Role of the Parish," in Nuesse and Harte (eds.) *The Sociology of the Parish* (Milwaukee: Bruce, 1951), ch. 12, made a zealous plea for convert-making. The problems of multiple roles and of role-conflict are a favorite theme of researchers in this area. See, for example, Fichter, *Religion as an Occupation*, ch. 6, "The Performance of Roles," and *Social Relations in the Urban Parish*, ch. 10, "Social Roles of the Parish Priest," and also the comparisons of ministers, priests and rabbis, under "Roles of the Clergy," pp. 216-238, in Salisbury, *Religion in American Culture*.

2. We did not ask questions about personal religious observances and practices, thus the data of this study do not provide the usual criteria for measuring exact parochial categories. Yet the assumption is safe that the priests had selected the parochial "inner circle" as respondents. For empirical qualifications of this category, see Fichter, *Social Relations in the Urban Parish*, ch. 3, "Nuclear Parishioners and Leaders." For some comparable data see Joseph B. Schuyler, *Northern Parish* (Chicago: Loyola University Press, 1960), *passim*.

3. "The big city parish almost defies the systematic visiting of homes. At best the priest can recognize names and addresses of parishioners. The tendency then is to visit no one unless an urgent problem is brought to light which requires the attention of a

priest." Dennis J. Geaney, *Christians in a Changing World* (Chicago: Fides, 1959), p. 163.

4. Some priests, like some parishioners, are more hospitable than others. In one parish a man said, "I've tried several times to see our parish priests, but never got beyond the secretary." In another parish, however, the remark was made that "the rectory door is always open, and that includes a cup of coffee if you feel like it."

5. Some of our informants believe that "the pastor has to be aloof from the people. He's the head man. It's the curate who should go out and mingle with the people."

6. One sympathetic woman feels that "educating the people to be more considerate of the priests is far better than establishing the cold system of office hours. Imagine Christ saying: 'Come and follow Me on Monday, Wednesday, and Friday, from 10 a.m. to 12 noon!' "

7. For seminarians' opinions about dating, see Fichter, *Religion as an Occupation,* pp. 43-46.

8. In a study of the Detroit area, Gerhard Lenski, *The Religious Factor* (Garden City: Doubleday, 1961), pp. 170-171, found that "involvement in the churches seems to have little relationship to the amount of thought given to world problems or to attitudes toward foreign aid. One might suppose that with important moral issues involved, participation in the churches would have some significant effect on people's thinking, but such is evidently not the case."

9. The fact that the parish priests do not rank Communism among the foremost problems of the Church in America seems to require some further analysis.

10. Fichter, "Anti-Clericalism in the American Catholic Culture," *The Critic,* vol. 21 (February-March, 1963), pp. 11-15.

11. For various estimates of Catholic college graduates see, for example, the Gaffin survey reported in the 1953 volume of *The Catholic Digest,* also Donald J. Bogue *The Population of the United States* (Glencoe: Free Press, 1959), pp. 688-710; and Bernard Lazerwitz, "Some Factors Associated with Variations in Church Attendance," *Social Forces,* vol. 39, no. 4 (May, 1961),

pp. 301-309; and "A Comparison of Major United States Religious Groups," *Journal of the American Statistical Association,* vol. 56, no. 295 (September, 1961), pp. 568-579. Based on the Gaffin study are the remarks of John L. Thomas, *Religion and the American People* (Westminster: Newman, 1963), pp. 124-127.
12. This sample is from Lazerwitz, "A Comparison of Major United States Religious Groups," *op. cit.,* p. 575. The fifteen percent at the bottom of the column "National Sample" includes those with no occupation. Irving Crespi, "Occupational Status and Religion," *American Sociological Review,* vol. 28, no. 1 (February, 1963), p. 131, gives the latest distribution used in Gallup Polls.

	White Protestants	White Catholics
Professional	11%	10%
Business	12	13
Clerical and sales	9	9
Skilled manual	17	20
Unskilled manual	13	20
Service and laborers	6	7
Farming	13	7
Non-labor force	18	12

13. This may be a partial explanation why the closest friends are less likely than the distant friends to say that the priest's main task is the financial management of the parish.

CHAPTER TWO

The College Graduate

Catholic priests generally have long been the best educated clergymen in the United States, the normal academic
seminary course requiring eight years beyond the high school
level.[1] The American Catholic laity, on the other hand, has
only in this generation reached the standard and amount of
education of non-Catholics. The Catholics of the United States
are no longer a poorly educated, low-income, immigrant population. Among the younger generation, Catholics now finish
high school and attend college in about the same proportions
as white Protestants and Jews.[2] Meanwhile, many priests,
especially those in the field of education, are going on for
graduate degrees beyond their usual professional theological
studies.

The friends of priests, who are the respondents to this study,
have a greater amount of schooling than the Catholic laity in
general. Thirty-five percent of them are college graduates.
They also demonstrate the inter-generational trend in the increase of education. Of those who are sixty years of age and
older, less than four out of ten (38%) went to college. Half
of the people in their forties, and more than six out of ten

(63%) of those who are in their thirties, attended college. All of these parishioners are twenty-five years of age and older, and are presumed to have finished their education.

TABLE 1—Percentage distribution of level of schooling attained by 2,216 parishioners.

No high school, or incomplete	14%
High school graduate	31
College incomplete	20
College graduate (or more)	35

The data of this study allow us to make some internal comparisons between parishioners with the least amount of schooling and those with the most schooling. Since education is an important social value in American society, we may readily make the assumption that important differences do exist between these two groups of parishioners. Beyond this general assumption, however, we are able to test out several related sub-hypotheses.

Pastors sometimes complain that college graduates are not good parishioners in the sense that they direct their apostolic interests and abilities to extra-parochial Catholic activities. It is sometimes said that the best educated people in the parish are highly critical of both the clergy and their fellow parishioners. There is also sometimes the feeling among the clergy, especially the older parish priests, that these college-bred men and women show a tendency toward "liberal" thinking and behavior.[3]

The basic comparison we are making here is between the parishioners who did not attend or did not finish high school, and those who attended college for four years but did not go on to graduate studies.[4] In order to isolate the factor of education as cleanly as possible, we have matched these two categories for age and sex. In order to obviate the influence of religious secondary training, we have paired the most educated —half of them having gone to Catholic high schools, and half to public high schools. This kind of refinement reduces the numbers of people in each category, so that we are here comparing 282 college graduates with 162 parishioners who have the least education.

There are, of course, other differences that are practically beyond statistical control but may indeed be a partial effect of the amount and kind of education these people have had. As expected, more of the college graduates (38%) than of the others (14%) report above-average income. The better educated include a larger proportion (18%) of unmarried persons than do the less educated (11%).[5] Those with the least education are more likely (30%) than the college people (15%) to live in a small place where there is a one-priest parish. The extent to which these factors of income, residential location, and marital status affect the attitudes of parishioners will be studied separately.[6]

Critics of the Priests

The first hypothesis we may test here is the complaint made by some pastors that educated Catholics are critical of the parish priest. Whether added schooling raises the expectations that Catholics have of their clergy, or whether it gives them a feeling of superiority over priests who have a different kind of education, can only remain an assumption at this point.[7] One of the consequences of college training is the sharpening of the critical faculties of man, but this should allow both positive appreciation as well as negative criticism.

TABLE 2—Comparative lay opinions of the preparations made by priests for their preaching.

	(162) Least Schooling	(282) College Graduates
Very well prepared	44%	18%
Fairly well prepared	44	48
More or less prepared	10	26
Poorly prepared	2	8

The college graduates are not nearly so content as the less educated with the sermons they have heard during the past year. This estimate does not concern the quality of preaching, but makes a judgment about the extent to which the preacher prepared his sermon. The people with the least amount of schooling are more than twice as willing (44%) as the college graduates (18%) to say that the sermons they have listened to have been "very well" prepared.

TABLE 3—Comparative estimates of priests' attitudes toward lay participation in the liturgy.

	(162) Least Schooling	(282) College Graduates
Very favorable	65%	54%
Quite favorable	22	28
Neutral about it	9	14
Opposed to it	4	4

Since there has been a great development in the liturgical movement during recent decades, the assumption is that priests are more and more in favor of the participation of the laity in the liturgy of the Church. The educated are probably more aware of this movement and its implication than are the others. They would probably expect more from the priests they know. Although the majority of all respondents say that priests have a favorable attitude on this question, the college graduates are considerably less reserved about giving a positive judgment.[8]

When we asked them what single change they would make to improve the parish in which they live, more of the poorly educated (14%) than of the well educated (6%) were satisfied to make no change at all. Both categories of parishioners, however, mentioned with greatest frequency the wish for more involvement of the laity in the operation of the parish. When we asked them about the advisability of occasional transfers for the parish clergy, six out of ten of the college graduates, as compared to less than half (48%) of the others, were in favor of this suggestion.

TABLE 4—Comparative estimates of work burdens on parish priests and on other professional men.

	(162) Least Schooling	(282) College Graduates
Priests' are heavier	51%	39%
About the same	33	40
Priests' are lighter	16	21

Since the better educated are more likely to be in a professional occupation, they are probably in a better position to make a valid judgment about the comparative job demands on priests and other professional men. An estimation of this kind, however, does not necessarily imply a negative criticism. The facts simply indicate that the less educated parishioners are more likely than the better educated to view the parish priest as a hard-working man.

In so far as these data allow us to draw a conclusion, they point clearly to the hypothesis that the best educated parishioners are more critical of the parish clergy. They do not think so highly of the sermons nor of the priests' attitude toward the laity in the liturgy. In general, they are less satisfied with the way the parish is run, and they are not so ready to believe that the priest is overworked.

Critics of the Parishioners

Are the college graduates more critical of the laity in the parish? One may well assume that if these well educated people find fault with the priest and the parish, they are likely also to be less tolerant of their fellow-parishioners. We have no way of knowing the extent to which they are personally involved in parish organizations, but we may surmise from the statements of many priests that these better educated persons do not cooperate well with parochial lay groups.

In their estimation of the lay leaders of parish groups these two categories of parishioners do not differ significantly. The overwhelming majority of both educated (86%) and least educated (88%) say that these lay leaders demonstrate a sense of responsibility when working with groups. The more educated are only slightly less willing (52%) than the poorly educated (56%) to remark that these lay leaders also exhibit the quality of initiative.

We asked them what kind of reaction is shown by the adult parishioners when an important program is being sponsored in the parish. Here we find a fairly significant difference of opinion between the better and the poorly educated. As a matter of fact, the college graduates are closer to the opinion of the parish priests themselves on this matter than they are to their fellow parishioners. Many more of them (21%) than of the less educated (5%) think that the adult parishioners are reluctant or indifferent to important parochial projects.

TABLE 5—Comparative judgments of the attitudes of parishioners to important parochial projects.

	(162) Least Schooling	(282) College Graduates	(2183) Priests
Eager and enthusiastic	31%	25%	21%
Fairly cooperative	64	54	61
Reluctant or indifferent	5	21	18

There is one other test question, the answers to which may be difficult of interpretation in relation to the hypothesis under discussion. In asking about the abilities of parish lay leaders and about the attitudes of adult parishioners, we were asking about factual information, that is, what these abilities and attitudes actually are. Now we asked them what *should be:* "In a parish organization, when a question comes up that does not concern faith or morals, which is the best position for the priest to take?"

TABLE 6—Preferable position for priest to take in discussions of parochial lay groups.

	(162) Least Schooling	(282) College Graduates
Equal vote with parishioners	22%	14%
Advice and counsel only	54	60
Power of veto and final decision	16	23
Complete control	8	3

The reasoning behind this question was that those who want
the priest to have complete control of lay groups are likely to
have little faith in the ability of parishioners to come to their
own decisions. On the other hand, those who want the priest
to have only an equal vote with the lay members are likely to
have greater faith in lay people. The odd comparative result
of this question is that the less educated check both of these
possibilities in greater proportions than do the college
graduates.[9]

In combining these various norms of comparison we do
not come to a completely definite conclusion on the proposed
hypothesis. Only on the question of parishioners' attitudes
toward important parish projects do we have a clear-cut difference that indicates a more critical attitude on the part of the
college graduates. All of these respondents are speaking about
conditions in their own home parish, and it is therefore difficult to draw generalizations about the normal, or average,
parish from what they say. If most of the parishioners are also
college graduates, then the opinions must be applied to a
specific kind of parish.

Progressive Parishioners

The third hypothesis we may suggest from these responses
is that the more educated the parishioner is, the more likely
will he be progressive and liberal in his social views. It is a
commonplace finding of social science research that increased
education in America tends to liberalize people.[10] This is not
shown here merely in the fact that more of the college graduates (38%) than of the others (9%) read the *Commonweal,*
or that more of them (37%) than of the less educated (7%)
read the *Atlantic Monthly.* The only periodical on the list

presented that is read more by the poorly schooled is the *Reader's Digest*.

One of the common tests of progressive social views is the question concerning attitudes towards America's foreign economic aid program. The majority of all respondents to this study, both priests and lay people, are in favor of either expanding or maintaining the program. In this instance, the distribution of opinion of the better educated lay persons is fairly close to that of the priests. As in many other questions that test the social awareness of American citizens, it is probably more significant to know the quality and kind of education, than the number of years of education, that an individual has had.

TABLE 7—Comparative attitudes toward the foreign economic aid program of the United States.

	(162) Least Schooling	(282) College Graduates	(2183) Priests
Expand the program	35%	44%	40%
Reduce it	36	32	33
Leave it as it is	27	23	24
No answer	2	1	3

While there are many exceptions to this generalization, one ordinarily thinks of the Democratic Party on the national scene at the present time as the more liberal of the major parties. It is said to attract intellectuals, a term that is not broad enough to include all those who have graduated from college. In the present study the indication is that economic status is a more significant factor in party preference than amount of schooling is. At any rate, the least educated respondents, who tend also to be of lower economic status, lean toward Democratic candidates (60%) much more than toward Republican (14%). Among the college graduates, who also enjoy higher income, the proportion favoring Democrats (43%) over Republicans (32%) is not nearly so large. The remainder in both educational categories claim to be independent voters.

TABLE 8—Comparative ranking of three most important social goals of the American people.

	(162) Least Schooling	(282) College Graduates	(2216) All Laity
Reducing crime and juvenile delinquency	41%	24%	29%
Securing basic rights of Americans regardless of race or creed	25	31	28
Reducing cold war tensions	14	22	21

What do these people think of the solution of social problems in the American society? The rank order of importance attributed to these social goals by the least and the most educated is probably not so significant as the proportionate distribution of opinions in each category. That those with least schooling vote so strongly on the matter of delinquency and so weakly on the matter of cold war tensions seems to bespeak a relatively restricted social orientation.[11] It is unquestionably true that increased years of education open a broader vista on the world's affairs. In every area in which we questioned them, except for sports and athletics, the college graduates indicate more interest and involvement than do the others.

The interpretation of these data is persuasive in the direction of the stated hypothesis that the better educated parishioners are more progressive and socially aware than their less educated fellows. While they favor Democratic national political candidates in about the same proportion as priests do (42%), they are twice as likely to vote Republican (32%) as are either the parish priests (15%) or the less educated lay people (14%) in the parish. This may well be a function of higher economic status rather than of greater education.

Extra-parochial Catholic

The college graduate tends to exercise his apostolic zeal outside his own parish. The evidence is relatively meager here, but the question seems worthy of testing since it touches upon a strongly held opinion among many parish priests. The logic behind this opinion is that people who attend colleges and universities—whether or not they leave their place of residence and their parish to do so—are drawn into a different level of activities, another circle of friends, and a broader milieu of thought. This experience supposedly alienates them more or less permanently from their parish.[12]

A larger proportion of the less educated (58%) than of the college graduates (51%) have a "best friend" among the clergy who is a pastor, while the others in both categories are better acquainted with a parochial curate. More of the college graduates (37%) are personally acquainted with the Bishop of their diocese. These facts, of course, provide only hints to the assumption that the college graduate's religious and ecclesiastical interests lie outside his own parish.

The parish priest visits the homes of the less educated more frequently than he does the homes of the college graduates. But there is a curious aspect to these visitations. When we

TABLE 9—Comparative frequency of home visits by the parish
        priest in past year.

	(162) Least Schooling	(282) College Graduates	(2216) Total Laity
Not at all	29%	38%	33%
Only once	20	14	18
Several times	30	29	30
Often	21	19	19

TABLE 10—Comparative frequency of home visits by non-parish
        priest.

	(162) Least Schooling	(282) College Graduates	(2216) Total Laity
Not at all	55%	38%	45%
Only once	11	14	12
Several times	24	34	29
Often	10	14	14

compared the purpose of the parish priest's visit, we found that
the call on the least educated is more often a friendly or social
one. A larger proportion of the college graduates (35%) than
of the least educated (24%) who had been visited by the
priest, said that he came there on "parish business." The implication may be that there are some parish leaders among the
college graduates, but that there are some close friends of the
priest among the least educated.

The most convincing indication of the college graduate's
extra-parochial interests lies in his contacts with priests who
come from outside his own parish. More than six out of ten of
them have had an "outside" priest visit in their home during
the year. We have seen that the closest friends of priests tend

to be at a somewhat higher economic level, and these college graduates also enjoy a higher income than the less educated. This does not explain, however, why the less educated have more visits from their parish priest, while the college graduates have more visits from priests who do not come from their parish. The explanation seems to lie in the fact that the college graduates simply have more friends and more interests outside the parish.

Summary

In reviewing the analysis of these data, it is clear that important differences exist between the best and the least educated of the nuclear parishioners. The caution must be made that other factors besides schooling are influential here: differences in income levels, residential location, and marital status. These variables, in some sense, are probably both cause and effect of the amount of education enjoyed by the parishioner. In spite of this, we have been able to control the factors of sex, age, and religious schooling in order to make a more reliable and logical comparison.

1. This information shows that college graduates tend to fit the image that many parish priests have of them. They are sharper in their criticism of the parish priest and his functions than is the case with the least educated.

2. College graduates also seem to be more critical of their fellow parishioners, although it cannot therefore be concluded that they take a more realistic view of the parochial milieu in general.

3. As may be expected, the college graduates have a somewhat more alert social orientation, and seem to be more interested in social issues and progress.

4. They are not so closely tied to the parish as are the less educated parishioners. They have wider interests and broader contacts with non-parish clergy, and this appears to be mainly the result of their college experience.

NOTES

1. In an otherwise excellent appraisal David Moberg is in error when he compares the amount of education enjoyed by clergymen. *The Church as a Social Institution*, pp. 486-487.
2. The most recent and reliable data on comparative education achievement have been analyzed by Andrew Greeley and others at the National Opinion Research Center of the University of Chicago. See his *Religion and Career* (New York: Sheed and Ward, 1963).
3. See references to this point in *Social Relations in the Urban Parish*, pp. 175-176. It may also be pointed out that the parish elementary school is often a magnet for parochial solidarity. See Fichter, *Parochial School: A Sociological Study* (Notre Dame: University of Notre Dame Press, 1958), pp. 433-435.
4. Twenty percent of the adult Catholics in the Detroit area studied by Gerhard Lenski, *The Religious Factor*, p. 236, attended or finished college. This is closer to the representative national statistics for Catholics, but considerably lower than the fifty-five percent of the present study.
5. This seems to be particularly the case with females, whose chances for marriage decline as their years of education increase. See Christopher Tietze and Patience Lauriat, "Age at Marriage and Educational Attainment in the United States," *Population Studies*, vol. 9, no. 2 (November, 1955), pp. 159-166; see also Paul Glick and Hugh Carter, "Marriage Patterns and Educational Level," *American Sociological Review*, vol. 23, no. 3 (June, 1958), pp. 294-300.
6. See the chapters, below, which treat these factors.
7. One of our informants, a well-educated businessman, claimed that

priests "suffer the narrowness of their specialized education—a problem that all professional men have."

8. A thirty-five year old male married teacher says that "minor orders should be held by laymen in the Church. Despite all arguments to the contrary, there is a need for the vernacular Mass. All one needs to be convinced is to attend an Episcopal Church service." For a brief modern treatment of this point, see J. A. Jungmann, "Liturgy in the Parish," pp. 64-71, in Hugo Rahner (ed.), *The Parish from Theology to Practice* (Westminster: Newman, 1958).

9. This was not the case in a study in Chile where the same question was asked. Thirty-seven percent of the college graduates said the priest should have an equal vote, and 17 percent of the least educated thought the priest should have complete control. See Fichter, *Cambio Social en Chile*, p. 161. Among Southern lay leaders males gave a stronger position to the priest than females did. See Fichter, *Social Relations in the Urban Parish*, p. 36.

10. That the more educated are also more tolerant to minority people is the thesis of John B. Holland, *Attitudes Toward Minority Groups in Relation to Rural Social Structure* (Unpublished dissertation, Michigan State University, 1950). See the evidence in Samuel A. Stouffer, *Communism, Conformity, and Civil Liberties* (New York: Doubleday, 1955), but also the remarks on "The Myth of College Liberalism," pp. 50-53, in Philip E. Jacob, *Changing Values in College* (New York: Harper Brothers, 1957).

11. Several studies have shown that "moral permissiveness," at least in attitudes toward others, increases with amount of schooling.

12. Although the apostasy rate increases with higher education, the University of Michigan Survey showed that "church attendance increases with increasing number of years of schooling for all Protestants and Catholics, Baptists and Methodists." See Bernard Lazerwitz, "Some Factors Associated with Variations in Church Attendance," *Social Forces*, vol. 39, no. 4 (May, 1961), p. 306, Table 5. The significant fact then is that Catholic college graduates are better Catholics but poorer parishioners.

CHAPTER THREE

Catholic High School Products

The friends of priests who cooperated in this study are generally better educated than the total American Catholic population. They are probably also more likely to have had a Catholic schooling. We did not ask them whether or not they attended parochial elementary school, but we did find that 750 of them attended a Catholic high school for four years, even more of them, 1,007, went exclusively to a public high school.[1] With the current pressures of students and finances on the Catholic school system, it is probable that this disproportion will increase, and that increasing numbers of young Catholics will attend public, or at least non-Catholic, high schools.

Taking the gross statistics of this survey we find practically no difference in the economic status of these two categories. Almost two-thirds of both (64%) say that their families are in the middle-income bracket, and three out of ten say that their income is above average. In gross comparison also, their marital status is about the same, about one out of six being still unmarried. Perhaps more unexpected is the fact that the products of Catholic high schools enter mixed marriages in about the same proportions (6-7%) as do the graduates of public high schools.

TABLE 1—Further education of graduates of Catholic and public
high schools.

	(750) Catholic	(1007) Public
Did not attend college	29%	42%
College incomplete	21	24
College graduate	50	34

Among the Catholic parishioners who are the friends of
priests, the graduates of Catholic high schools attend and
finish college in higher proportions than do the public high
school graduates. Since these people are highly selective,
however, and also represent a considerable age-range, it is not
possible to extend this statement to the general Catholic population of high school graduates. This is not, of course, a comparison between Catholics and people of other religions, nor
between the total products of Catholic and public high
schools.[2] Such comparisons have been made in other places,
and they show quite clearly that there no longer exists in
America the religious difference in amount of education
among young adults.[3]

TABLE 2—Sex comparison in higher education of graduates of
Catholic and public high schools.

	Catholic High		Public High	
	(447) Male	(303) Female	(562) Male	(445) Female
Did not attend college	18%	45%	33%	53%
College incomplete	20	23	20	29
College graduate	62	32	47	18

In this total study we find that those who attended Catholic
high school for four years were more likely (71%) to go to

college than were those (58%) who went four years to public
high school. Half of the former completed college, as compared to one-third of the latter. Males in both categories are
much more likely than females to have attended, and also to
have finished, college; but even in this comparison, the male
from the Catholic high school is much more likely (62%)
than the male from the public high school (47%) to have
completed his college education.[4]

The hypothesis may be suggested that the family sending
its child to a Catholic high school is financially better off than
the family sending its child to the free, tax-supported public
school. The present data, however, show a remarkable similarity of income status between these two categories of respondents. The significant difference is between the sexes
within each category. In so far as economic status is a factor
in educational opportunities, it seems to affect the female's
chances of higher education, and not her chances of going
to a Catholic rather than a public high school.

TABLE 3—Sex comparison in income status of graduates of Catholic and public high schools.

	Catholic High		Public High	
	(447)	(303)	(562)	(445)
	Male	*Female*	*Male*	*Female*
Above average	35%	22%	36%	18%
Average income	60	69	58	75
Below average	5	9	6	7

Matched Sample

In an attempt to isolate and measure the factor of Catholic
high school education, we selected only those respondents

who had finished high school but had not gone on to college. This reduced the number considerably, but then we felt that we had to control certain other variables. For example, the two groups are matched exactly on the age factor,[5] and also on marital status.

This refinement, control, and matching of variables leaves us with 162 Catholic high school graduates, and exactly the same number of public high school graduates. Other life experiences are obviously influential on present behavior and attitudes, as may be seen from the other kinds of comparative analysis made in this study. The present comparison, however, allows us to focus sharply on the single and central factor: the differential influence of Catholic and public high school experience.

The Catholic high school graduates tend to come in higher proportions from the Midwest, and in lower proportions from the Northeast and the Pacific Coast. This clearly reflects differential regional availability of Church high schools. None of the Catholic high graduates is a convert, as compared to 17 percent of the public high graduates. The lack of college education in their parents is approximately the same, less than one in ten of the parents having attended college.

Clergy-Lay Relations

As may be expected, the products of Catholic high schools have closer personal relations with the clergy, but this does not refer to the priests in their own parish. About seven out of ten of both categories say that the parish priest has been in their home during the previous year, but the purpose of the priestly visit is somewhat different. One-third of the Catholic schoolers, as compared to one-fifth (22%) of the others, report that their parish priest makes social calls to their homes.

The graduates of Catholic high schools apparently have a much broader acquaintance with the clergy since more than half (54%) of them, as compared to four out of ten (39%) of the others, entertained non-parochial priests in their homes. This is indicative of the fact that few Catholic high schools are parish-operated and that the students who attend these schools learn to associate with religious order priests who run the schools. Parish priests sometimes make the same complaint in this regard that they do in reference to college students— that the individual's interest in parochical activities is lessened when he is drawn away for academic purposes.

Except for one or two items, the products of both types of high school education tend to have the same cordial attitudes toward the clergy. The Catholic school graduates are considerably more critical of the sermons they hear in Church, and it may be that their religious education has raised their expectations in this regard. On the other hand, they also express a greater appreciation of the "hard work" that a parish priest has to do, in comparison with other professional men.

In another study of Catholic young men in the armed services, we found that six out of ten Catholic high graduates, as compared to only one-third of the public high graduates, had once thought about studying for the priesthood. In the same study we found that more of the former (83%) than of the latter (56%) said that they had had fairly close contact with priests and religious Brothers or Sisters.[6]

There seems to be no doubt that the experience of a Catholic high school education is a factor in developing and maintaining good relations between the clergy and the laity. It does not necessarily develop a greater spirit of loyalty to the Church. In our nation-wide study of Catholic young men, we found no difference in response to this question between those who went to Catholic high schools and those who did not. But the abstract image of the Church, to which a person expresses fealty, is not the same as the image of the clergy, with whom the respondent has personal contact. It is apparent that an individual can be true to the Church and still not appreciate the priests he knows.

Better Educated

Aside from the fact that Catholic high school graduates have closer, friendly relations with the clergy, can they also be said to have a "better" education? Since we have excluded those who went on to college, we know that the completion of high school ended their formal educational training. What about their wider interests, for example, their reading habits which must have been influenced by their educational background? Both kinds of graduates, in about the same proportion, say that they have increased their interest in reading for information during the past decade. The public school graduate, however, is more likely to have increased his habit of reading for relaxation.

When tested on a series of current periodicals, both categories of respondents indicate that they do about the same amount of reading, but there is a difference in the specific periodicals they read. The public school graduates read the *Atlantic Monthly*; but the Catholic school graduates read *America* and *Commonweal* more. This difference is probably expected since these Catholic magazines are not so likely to be present in the libraries of public schools. The Catholic school graduates include a larger percentage of readers of *Time* maga-

ine, while the public school graduates include more readers of
Life, Reader's Digest, and the *Saturday Evening Post.*

TABLE 4—Comparative proportions of Catholic and public high
graduates who have increased their interest and involvement in selected areas.

	(162) Catholic	(162) Public
International affairs	62%	69%
Race relations	52	51
Management-Labor relations	43	49
Religious issues	42	54
Community organization	31	41
Athletic events	13	19
Music, art, theater	11	17

We know from other research that the product of the
Catholic school understands his religion better, that is, he
knows the doctrine, the prayers, and the Commandments,
that are part of his religious education. What seems of great
pertinence in the present study, however, is that a larger
proportion of public school graduates have increased their
interest in religious issues during the past ten years. One can
only speculate whether the product of the Catholic school feels
that he has had "enough religion" once he has finished his
formal education.

Social Awareness

The series of social issues or areas, indicated in Table 4,
shows differences in matters other than religious issues. The
public school products demonstrate more interest and involvement in the problems of management and labor. They are

much more involved in civic and community organizations. They also take a greater interest in the various "cultural" activities like music, theater, and the arts, and even in athletic contests and events.

Other items in this study indicate agreement on the social alertness and attitudes of these respondents. For example, there is no difference in their degree of interest in the problem of American race relations. The type of high school they attended does not seem to have had a differential effect on their political preference and affiliation. Six out of ten of both categories say that they lean toward Democratic candidates in national elections; eighteen percent favor the Republicans, and the rest claim to be independent voters.[7]

From a broader perspective we presented to them a series of eight social goals about which Americans have been frequently concerned. We asked them to check those which they consider the most important. The graduates of Catholic schools ranked in first place the reduction of crime and delinquency, in second place the securing of the basic rights of all Americans, regardless of creed or race, and in third place reducing the tensions of the cold war. The public school graduates agree that these are the three most important goals of our society, but they rank the securing of citizens' basic rights of greater importance than the reduction of crime and delinquency.

The slight but consistent disparity of social awareness between the graduates of Catholic and public high schools is not easily explained. Perhaps a more intriguing question is why these differences are not greater—and in the other direction. For example, it is difficult to understand why a larger proportion of public school graduates (45%) than of Catholic school graduates (28%) are in favor of expanding the foreign economic aid program of the United States. More of the Catholic school products (43%) than of the public school graduates (35%) are in favor of reducing it. The remainder in both categories want to leave the program as it is. This difference of opinion may be partly explained by the fact that a larger proportion of public school respondents expresses a growing interest in international affairs.

We must remember that these two categories are matched for sex and age, and that none of these people went to college. In another study, of male college students in Louisiana, we found quite the reverse. The graduates of Catholic high schools were more liberal in their political views, more socially alert and progressive, than the public high school graduates. But this is a local situation in which the freedom to teach the social doctrines of the Church and the values of Americanism is broad in the Catholic school system, and narrowly restricted in the public school system.

In the nation-wide study of the friends of priests, the consistent difference between the Catholic and the public school graduates is not the result of statistical chance. It is not a local or regional phenomenon since our sample represents adequately all dioceses of the United States. The public school products seem to be more progressive and alert, more interested in the activities of their fellowman and in the welfare of society.

At this stage of research in the cooperative school systems we can merely speculate about explanations. Perhaps the content of the courses in the public high schools covers a wider range of information and interest. Perhaps the extra-curricular activities of the student body have a more broadening effect. Perhaps the background training and educational outlook of

the public school teachers are more humane and social than
those of the Catholic school teachers.

Summary

The comparison of the Catholic school system with any
other system of education must be made with great caution.
The central problem is the attempt to isolate the factor of
education and measure its effect on the lives of people. Like
most sociological analyses, this one is involved in multiple
and complex factors and motivations. Many other elements
besides formal schooling account for the behavior of people.

1. In the total study, the graduates of the two different
kinds of high schools represent approximately the same economic or income status, and have about the same proportions
in Catholic and in mixed marriages, and unmarried persons.
Females in both groups, however, report themselves in lower
income brackets.

2. The Catholic high school graduates are much more
likely to attend and finish college than are the graduates of
public high schools. Here again, there is a significant difference across sex lines; the women in both categories are less
likely to have finished their college education.

3. When we eliminate those with college experience and
matched the others exactly on age, sex, and marital status,
we find that the products of Catholic high schools have closer
personal relations with the clergy, even though they are more
critical of preaching, than is the case with the public high
school graduates.

4. Whether the Catholic high school graduate received a
"better" education is not so easy to determine. He knows
Christian doctrine and prayers better, and reads Catholic

periodicals more frequently, but his post-graduate interest in religious issues has not increased as much as that of the public school graduate.

5. In the broader areas of social consciousness the public high school graduate seems to be more alert and progressive than the Catholic high school graduate. This is shown in the extent to which they take interest in various social issues and favor the more liberal and progressive social programs and movements.

NOTES

1. These materials were discussed in an article, "Catholics and High School," *America*, vol. 107, no. 124 (September 15, 1962), pp. 718-721.
2. According to a study in 1961, almost fifty percent of the public high school students entered college. See National Education Association, Research Division, *Studies of High School Graduates* (Washington, D. C., January, 1962), reported under the same title in *NEA Research Bulletin,* vol. 40, no. 2 (May, 1962), pp. 42-45. It is generally assumed among educators that ten percent more of the private and Catholic high school graduates go to college.
3. Attention was drawn to this point in Fichter, *Religion as an Occupation,* pp. 65f. See also the findings of Andrew Greeley, *Religion and Career* (New York, Sheed and Ward, 1963).
4. More girl seniors in high school than boys plan to attend college, but fewer girls than boys actually finish college. See the article, "College Attendance and Youth," *NEA Research Bulletin,* vol. 40, no. 1 (February, 1962), pp. 18-21, which summarizes a study published by the Bureau of the Census in August 1961.
5. The factor of age is extremely important because younger Catholics have more education than older Catholics. In the present study less than 5 percent (4.5%) of those in the 25-29 years age group did not attend or did not finish college, as compared to 40 percent among the respondents sixty years of age or older.

6. This unpublished study on trainees in the armed services showed that the three influential factors of clergy contact, Catholic schooling, and religious parents, effected different results in the religious behavior and attitude of these young men.

7. This is at variance with the findings of Lenski, *op. cit.*, p. 249, who observes that "a Catholic education increased the probability of Catholics being Republicans. This is, of course, consistent with our earlier finding that involvement in the Church, measured by attendance at Mass and participation in church-related organizations, increased the probability of Catholics being Republicans."

CHAPTER FOUR

Social Class and Anti-Clericalism

In spite of the predictions of secularists and the warnings of religious conservatives, scientific research in general indicates that clergy-lay relations in all American religions are more cordial than they have ever been since the time of the original colonies. The prestige of the clergy, as reflected by the general attitudes of the American population, has risen even higher since the Second World War. Religion, and the functionaries of religion, have probably never been so popular as they are at the present time.[1] This does not mean, of course, that there are no irreligious and anti-religious Americans, or that everybody likes all of the priests, ministers, and rabbis of the nation.

The attempt to search out the degree of anti-clericalism existing in a population requires a fairly clear definition of the term. A person who is opposed to all forms of religion is obviously opposed to the professional representatives of religion.[2] A person who says, "I like Catholics, but I don't like priests and bishops," is certainly anti-clerical. A Catholic who complains that the clergy is domineering, authoritarian, selfish, and power-hungry, would at best be called unsympathetic, but is most likely a typical anti-clerical.[3]

Criticism of the clergy is not unknown among faithful Catholics, and criticism is a relative attitude. The norms of criticism may be quite objective, for example, the person who complains about the sermons preached in his parish Church may have good reason for the complaint—if it is a fact that the parish priest is a poor preacher. Indeed, in the present study we have found that the priests are more critical of their own sermons than the lay people are, and one would hardly call a priest anti-clerical.

This relativity of judgment is the hypothesis we are testing at this point. We make the assumption that some kinds of Catholics are more critical of the clergy than others are. The people who are here giving their opinions are recognized as good, practicing Catholics. They are active, cooperative people who know the most about the parish and the parish priests. The information they have provided allows us to test the hypothesis that upper-class people are more critical, and lower-class people least critical, of the parish clergy.[4]

In order to isolate exactly the factor of social class, we have controlled and matched the sex and age of respondents. There is an equal proportion of males and females in each of the three social classes, and the age range is the same in each. The three available norms for social class are income, education, and occupation.[5] People who have graduated from college, enjoy above average income derived from professional and executive occupation, we term upper-class. At the other pole, in the lower class, are those who have not attended or not finished high school, who have median and below average income, derived from the lower white-collar and blue-collar occupations.

The upper-class people have a smaller percentage (12%) of converts to Catholicism than do the lower-class (17%).

The married people in the upper class tend to be more often (10%) in mixed marriages than are those in the lower class (5%). On the other hand more of the lower class (33%) than of the upper class (11%) live in small-town, one-priest parishes; and this may partly account for the fact that more of the lower class (59%) than of the upper (52%) say that their best friend among the parish clergy is a pastor.

Proximity to Clergy

All of the respondents to this study are fairly well acquainted with the parish clergy, and seven out of ten in all three social classes say that the priest they know best has a cheerful and happy personality. About half of them in all three classes report that their parish priest has visited their home several times, or often, during the past year. The upper-class people, however, are twice as likely (60%) as the lower class (31%) to have had a visit from a non-parish priest during this same period.

TABLE 1—Class distribution of people who have been visited by priest several times, or often, in last year.

	(200)	(410)	(200)
	Upper	Middle	Lower
Parish priest visitor	53%	50%	54%
Non-parish priest	60	36	31
Either or both	81	67	63

Research studies in general indicate that lower-class people tend to have fewer friends and acquaintances than do the people in the middle and upper classes.[6] This generalization extends to friendships between the clergy and laity. The data show that the upper-class circle of priest friends is much wider than that of the middle and lower classes. When the statistics are combined, we find that eight out of ten of the upper-class respondents have had either a parish priest or a non-parish priest (or both) in their homes during the past year. On this basis alone, the suggestion may be made that upper-class Catholics are more friendly with the clergy, and thus not likely to be anti-clerical.

TABLE 2—Purpose of parish priests' visits to respondents' homes by social class.

	(200) Upper	(410) Middle	(200) Lower
Spiritual or sick call	12%	11%	21%
Social or parish reason	56	57	53
No visits	32	32	26

There is a hint in these comparative data that the parish priest visits the lower-class family more often for the purpose of spiritual and sacerdotal ministration. This appears to be the main reason why fewer (26%) of the lower class than of the upper class (32%) said that their parish priest had not visited them at all during the year. As a further index of proximity to the clergy, we find that slightly more (36%) of the upper class than of the lower class (30%) have met, talked with, or are good friends of the bishop of their diocese.

Attitudes toward the Seminary

Catholics who are favorably inclined toward the Church and its priests are usually interested also in the problem of vocations to the priesthood. When we asked these respondents what they considered the most serious problem facing the Church in America, the middle-class parishioners rated the shortage of Church vocations in first place, Communism in second place, and general religious indifference in third. The lower class put Communism in first place, lack of vocations in second, and indifference in third. The upper class puts the school problem first, lack of apostolic laity second, and relations with non-Catholics third.

The point of interest here is twofold. None of these people even mention anti-clericalism as a problem to the Church in America. They do not recognize its existence. In regard to the shortage of vocations, the upper class does not consider this among the three main problems of the Church, while the middle class gives it the first rank, and the lower class the second. The priests themselves, with whom the upper class associates most, put the vocation problem in third place, after religious indifference and the school problem.

TABLE 3—Class distribution of responses to whether priest friend encourages boys to enter the seminary.

	(200) Upper	(410) Middle	(200) Lower
Much or quite a bit	55%	67%	76%
More or less	35	26	19
Little or not at all	9	6	3

In the judgment of the respondents to this study, the kinds of priests with whom the upper-class people associate are not so intent upon encouraging vocations to the seminary as are the priests with whom the lower class associates. If one takes it as an objective norm that all priests should try to send boys to the seminary, the judgment of the upper class may be considered a criticism of the priests. On the basis of other questions, however, there does appear a sharp class difference of opinion about the seminary.

TABLE 4—Class distribution of advice to 13-year old boy who wants to become a priest.

	(200) Upper	(410) Middle	(200) Lower	(2183) Priests
Enter minor seminary now	25%	49%	50%	53%
Finish high school first	59	44	43	41
Finish college first	11	3	0	2
Consult spiritual director	5	4	7	4

The upper-class people show much less faith than do the others in the advisability of sending a young boy for his high school training to a minor seminary.[7] Perhaps because of their broader education, or their wider experiences, or their contacts with non-parish priests, seven out of ten of them feel that a boy should finish either high school or college before entering the seminary. The opinions of the middle and lower classes are much closer to those of the priests we queried, about half of

TABLE 5—Class differences of advice on social relations of high school senior who thinks he has a vocation.

	(200) Upper	(410) Middle	(200) Lower	(2183) Priests
Give up or limit parties and dating	19%	28%	34%	38%
Continue parties but discontinue dating	26	25	21	36
Do as other Catholic boys his age do	49	41	41	23
Other advice	6	6	4	3

whom (53%) think that the young boy should enter the minor seminary immediately after elementary school.

The upper-class people have a more "liberal" attitude toward the high school senior who is thinking about entering the seminary. Only one-fifth of them would have him limit or change the normal social life of a high school boy. The lower class is closer to the opinion of priests in this regard. In general, however, the priests, who may be presumed to know best the preparation needed before entrance to the seminary, differ considerably from the lay respondents on this question. It is not necessarily suggestive, however, that a difference of opinion on this matter implies anti-clericalism on the part of the laity.

Appraisal of Clergy's Work

The lay people who look at the kinds of functions that the parish priest performs rate them in approximately the same way, regardless of class distinctions. All three social classes believe that finances and administration take most of the priest's time, that counselling people is second, and that directing lay organizations is third. We did not ask them to evaluate these functions, but simply to indicate those that were most time-consuming.

There is somewhat less agreement, but not much, on the suggestion that parish priests should have office hours for their appointments. Slightly less than half of the respondents in all classes approve this suggestion, but more of the middle and lower class disapprove it. It may be pointed out here, however, that the laity are about twice as likely to approve this arrangement as are the priests themselves.

TABLE 6—Class distribution of opinions concerning the establishment of office hours for the parish priest.

	(200) Upper	(410) Middle	(200) Lower	(2183) Priests
Favorable	50%	46%	47%	25%
Neutral	28	21	20	12
Disapprove	22	33	33	63

The priests are much more unfavorable to the suggestion of
office hours than the lay people are favorable to it. Both are
looking at this question from different points of view, and it is
one of the areas of this study in which disagreement between
clergy and laity is greatest. In two other comparative items,
however, we find the laity more sympathetic to the priests than
the priests are to themselves.

TABLE 7—Class distribution of opinions on occupational demands
made on priests and other professional men.

	200) Upper	(410) Middle	(200) Lower	(2183) Priests
Priests work harder	32%	48%	52%	33%
About the same	42	35	34	32
Not so hard	26	17	14	35

TABLE 8—Class distribution of opinions on the "worries" of priests
compared to those of married men.

	(200) Upper	(410) Middle	(200) Lower	(2183) Priests
Priests' are heavier	39%	50%	58%	18%
About the same	29	26	23	19
Lighter	32	24	19	63

Middle and lower class people are much more sure, than priests and upper class people, that the parish priest has to work harder than other professional men in the American society.[8] Priests are almost evenly divided into three categories in their opinions on this subject, but they are much closer to agreement with upper class people than they are with the other lay persons.

The question whether the parish priest's "worries" are heavier than those of married men reveals a great range of responses. Here again the middle and lower class people are much more sympathetic to the priests in this regard. Perhaps the upper class is much more realistic in their judgment about the worries of priests, but they are still twice as likely (39%) as are the priests themselves (18%) to say that these worries are greater than those of married men. The priests are three times as likely (63%) as are the lower class people (19%) to say that the priests' worries are lighter than the married men's.[9]

Dissatisfaction with Clergy

One of the comments that might be termed an anti-clerical complaint, heard perhaps in countries that are poorer than the United States, is that the clergy is "living too well." This refers to the housing and the material standard of living that the priests enjoy. Since living quarters are supplied by the parish, and since parishes throughout the country range from wealthy to poor, it is to be expected that there are also great differences in the living standards of the parish clergy. In this total study the majority (55%) of the laity think that the parish priest lives at about the same level that they do. The rest are evenly divided, saying that the priest lives better than they do (23%) or that he lives more poorly than they (22%).

TABLE 9—Class distribution of estimates of lay respondents' standard of living compared to that of priests'.

	(200) Upper	(410) Middle	(200) Lower	(2216) Total Laity
Higher than priests'	44%	14%	12%	22%
About the same	48	58	51	55
Lower than priests'	8	29	37	23

Since the economic status of the individual is an important criterion of social class, we may well expect that upper class people live better than the clergy and that lower class people live more poorly than the clergy. The data confirm this expectation in general, but they show also that the largest group within each social class says that the parish priest lives at about the same level that they do.

Another means of discerning satisfaction or dissatisfaction with the clergy is through the suggestion of changes that the respondent thinks should be made in the parish where he lives. More of the lower class (26%) than of the middle class (15%) or the upper class (13%) are either satisfied, or can suggest no improvement. More of the upper class (20%) than of the middle (16%) or the lower (15%) want changes that would increase lay participation in the parish. About 7 percent in all classes would like to have the present pastor removed. These are probably the most dissatisfied of all parishioners even though their antipathy is probably directed at one priest rather than at the clergy in general.

TABLE 10—Class distribution of opinions on whether parish
   priests should be occasionally transferred.

	(200)	(410)	(200)
	Upper	*Middle*	*Lower*
Transfer pastors, not curates	2%	7%	10%
Transfer curates, not pastors	24	21	16
Transfer both	27	22	19
Transfer neither	46	50	53

The lower class people are generally more in favor (53%) than are the upper class (46%) of keeping parish priests on a permanent basis. On the other hand, one-tenth of the lower class favor the transfer of pastors. Since we asked no explanation of these opinions, we can only surmise whether this involves criticism of the clergy. The lay people may well believe that experience in a variety of parishes is of great value in the parochial ministry, especially for younger curates.

Certain class differences show up in the opinions people have about the sermons they hear. Fewer of the upper class (32%) than of the middle (41%) or of the lower (47%) are ready to say that the sermons they have heard in the past year seem to be "very well prepared." In this regard the laity has a higher regard for the sermons than the priests do, only one-fifth of whom say that their sermons are very well prepared.

A class difference of opinion is seen also in the question of clerical attitudes toward the participation of the laity in the liturgy.[10] Four out of ten (42%) of the upper class, as compared to more than half (54%) of the middle, and two-thirds of the lower class, say that the priest they know best is "very much" in favor of such lay participation. Less than one-fifth

(18%) of the priests give this much credit to their fellow
clergymen.

TABLE 11—Class distribution of opinions on extent to which
parish priests favor lay participation in the liturgy.

	(200) Upper	(410) Middle	(200) Lower	(2183) Priests
Very favorable	42%	54%	66%	18%
Quite favorable	29	29	23	40
Neutral	24	14	9	35
Opposed	5	3	2	7

Differences on Social Attitudes

The social class to which one belongs is generally conceded
to be one of the important determinants of the kinds of social
attitudes that people have. While the class "struggle" never
developed in America in the way that Marxists predicted it,
there is nevertheless a much greater class consciousness than
most Americans want to admit. In the present study, for
example, we may surmise that if the Catholic priests identify
themselves more with one class than with another, there may
be expected some antagonism among the people in the class
that the clergy neglects.

TABLE 12—Class distribution of respondents' preference for national political candidates.

	200) Upper	(410) Middle	(200) Lower	(2183) Priests
Leaning toward Democrats	37%	61%	64%	42%
Toward Republicans	39	21	10	15
Independent voters	23	18	24	40

There is no question that American Catholics favor the Democratic candidates on the national scene, but the influence of class position is clearly seen in the present data. The upper-class respondents tend to break away from this Catholic generalization. They are four times as likely as the lower class, and twice as likely as the middle class, to prefer Republican candidates.[11] The clergy is more Democratic than the upper class and more Republican than the lower class, but this does not identify them with the middle class. The priests are twice as likely as the middle class to be independent voters. The scientific problem here seems to be that we are dealing with priests as though they constitute a single "class" with its own social attitudes.

TABLE 13—Class distribution of attitudes on the foreign economic aid program of the United States.

	(200)	(410)	(200)	(2183)
	Upper	*Middle*	*Lower*	*Priests*
Favor expanding it	40%	39%	30%	40%
Favor reducing it	34	36	34	33
Leave as it is	24	24	33	24

The question of foreign economic aid, which has become one of the sharpest criteria for distinguishing the "liberals" from the "conservatives" at the present time, shows a remarkable similarity of opinion between the clergy and the laity and among the three social classes. The comparative data show that one-third of all of these categories is in favor of reducing the foreign aid program. The lower class is more in favor of maintaining the program than of expanding it, but this must be considered in itself a positive social attitude.

The way in which people rank the important social goals

TABLE 14—Class distribution of opinions concerning the importance of selected social goals.

	(200) Upper	(410) Middle	(200) Lower	(2183) Priests
Reduction of crime and delinquency	25%	32%	42%	34%
Securing basic rights of all Americans	26	28	20	31
Reduction of cold war tensions	26	21	15	5

of American society is probably also a function of their class position. In a series of eight proposed social goals about which Americans are concerned, the lower class was much more likely than the others to put in first place the reduction of crime and delinquency. The upper class is much more likely than the lower class to emphasize the importance of "cold war" tensions. In ranking the problem of crime first, and civil rights second, the priests are fairly similar to the middle class, but they differ sharply from the lay people in ranking the problems of mental illness, urban congestion, and public schools above the problem of the cold war.

TABLE 15—Class distribution of respondents who have increased their interest in various social issues.

	(200) Upper	(410) Middle	(200) Lower	(2183) Priests
International affairs	66%	63%	53%	49%
Race relations	64	56	48	43
Labor relations	51	51	39	34
Community organization	44	38	33	33
Music, art, theater	26	16	15	22

A consistent class differential is demonstrable in the degree to which respondents show increased interest in various social areas of American life. Except on the matter of labor relations, in which the upper and middle class indicate the same degree of increased interest, the upper class shows higher proportions on every item. With the exception of interest in music, art, and theater, the clergy show themselves closer to the lower class than to the others. The obvious expectation here is that the priests would be similar in their interests to the better educated, professional people in the upper class.

Summary

Although the laity differs from the clergy in many respects, and the social classes of Catholics differ from one another, there is no clear evidence of anti-clericalism among these respondents. Thus there is no support for the popular thesis that as American Catholics become better educated and achieve economic success, they alienate themselves from the Catholic clergy. We have been able to supply comparative data from priest respondents in many instances and are thus able to indicate some generalizations across clergy-lay lines as well as across class lines.

1. Upper class Catholics have more contact with non-parochial priests, and they show less concern for the vocation problem than do the other lay people. They are less in favor of sending a young boy to the minor seminary, and are more lax in social expectations of pre-seminary boys than are the clergy or the other laity.

2. On their appraisal of the parish priests' functions, the laity generally are more sympathetic to the priests than the priests are to themselves. They think the priests work harder

than they do, and that they worry more than they actually do. In these two items, however, the upper-class Catholics tend to have a more realistic opinion—in that it agrees more closely with the priests' opinion—than is the case in the middle and lower classes. On the matter of office hours for the parish priest, all classes of the laity differ sharply from the opinion of the clergy.

3. In some areas the upper class show themselves more critical of the clergy. They have a lower estimation of the sermons they hear, and they also think less of the clergy's willingness to involve the laity in the liturgy. The critical attitudes of the upper class are shown also in the fact that more of them are ready to suggest changes to be made in the parish where they live, and that they are more willing to have the parish priests transferred occasionally. There is no evidence that these friends of priests, regardless of their class position, are negatively critical of the material standards of living of the parish priests.

4. People who share the same interests and attitudes are probably most often in sympathy with one another. The laity of all classes are similar to the priests in their opinions about foreign economic aid. The upper class, however, leans much more to the Republican party than do the clergy or the laity in the middle and lower classes. The upper class does not emphasize the problems of crime and delinquency, but it does emphasize more the importance of "cold war" tensions. Finally, the upper class is most dissimilar to the clergy in the various areas of social interests. In this regard, the parish clergy show themselves closer to the interests of the lower class than to those of the middle and upper classes.

NOTES

1. See this point in Fichter, *Are We Going Secular?* (Milwaukee: Marquette University Press, 1960), pp. 17f.; also the oft-cited Roper Polls as discussed by Will Herberg, *Protestant-Catholic-Jew* (New York: Doubleday, 1955), p. 64, and the rating comparisons in Bernard Barber, *Social Stratification* (New York: Harcourt, Brace, 1957), pp. 100ff., and an earlier study by Murray Leiffer, *The Layman Looks at the Minister* (New York: Abingdon-Cokesbury, 1947).

2. Sometimes these are the consequence of professional misunderstanding, as occurs in the relationship between clergymen and social workers, with anti-secularism on one side and anti-clericalism on the other. For a case in point see David O. Moberg and Russell H. Vought, "The Minister and Social Work," *The Midwest Sociologist,* vol. 19, no. 1 (December, 1956), pp. 38-44.

3. The kinds of charges made in Paul Blanshard, *American Freedom and Catholic Power* (Boston: Beacon Press, 1949) and similar writings, bespeak more anti-clericalism than anti-Catholicism. It tends, indeed, to be the thesis of such propagandists that the Catholic laity are fine people—the trouble lies with the clergy.

4. It has become commonplace, especially for non-Catholic observers, to remark that "the upper-income, well-educated Catholic laymen are much less receptive to clerical guidance as to the practical social implications of moral and religious laws of the church than are the lower-income, more poorly educated Catholics." See Kenneth W. Underwood, *Protestant and Catholic* (Boston: Beacon Press, 1957), p. 94. Most recent happenings in Southern race relations call this kind of generalization into question in all religious bodies. "Indeed in the years after 1954 the cleavage between rank-and-file communicants and denominational leaders widened markedly," says Kenneth K. Bailey, *Southern White Protestantism* (New York: Harper & Row, 1964), p. 145.

5. Class criteria are more numerous than this, even in the relatively simple stratification system. See Fichter, *Sociology* (Chicago: University of Chicago Press, 1957), ch. 2, "Social Status." For an excellent recent summary see Gerhard Lenski, "Social Stratifica-

tion," pp. 521-538, in Joseph C. Roucek, (ed.), *Readings in Contemporary American Sociology* (Paterson: Littlefield, Adams, 1961).

6. See the analysis of such data by Genevieve Knupfer, "Portrait of the Underdog," *Public Opinion Quarterly,* vol. xi (Spring, 1947), pp. 103-114.

7. There is ample evidence that Catholic boys from better-income families tend to delay their entrance into the seminary. See Fichter, *Religion as an Occupation* (Notre Dame: University of Notre Dame Press, 1961), pp. 84f.

8. One middle-aged business woman said "the priests always seem to be busy, and they're always groaning how busy they are. It makes the lay people feel uncomfortable when they want to see the priest who is always in a hurry."

9. A parishioner who is a lower-class sympathetic man, remarked that "a married man has one to argue with. The poor pastor has hundreds." See the comments of Donald J. Thorman, *The Emerging Layman* (Garden City: Doubleday, 1962), ch. 2, "The New Look in Clergy-Lay Relations."

10. An upper-class male parishioner says: "To me, the lack of vocations, absence of the laity at some liturgical functions, failure to take more community responsibility, are due mainly to an inability of the laity to feel a real part of the Church as an organization." See the similar sentiments expressed by Daniel Callahan, *The Mind of the Catholic Layman* (New York: Scribner's, 1963), ch. 6, "Concord and Conflict: Clergy and Laity."

11. Catholics are also more faithful to Church attendance as their class position improves. Several studies have shown that Church-going people tend to vote Republican more than those who go to Church infrequently. For data on Protestants, see Morris Janowitz and Dwaine Marvick, *Competitive Pressure and Democratic Consent* (Ann Arbor: Institute of Public Administration, 1956), p. 27. For data on Detroit Catholics, see Lenski, *The Religious Factor,* ch. 4, "Religion and Politics." The curious possibility for the future is that higher social status and greater fidelity to Church attendance may both be correlates of Catholics switching from Democrats to Republicans.

CHAPTER FIVE

Marriage and Settling Down

Family folklore in America includes the commonplace observation that marriage has a "sobering" effect on young people, that they settle down to heavier responsibilities, recognize their greater stake in the community, and tend to become conservative in their thinking. The adaptation and compatibility that are required in the new relationship between husband and wife, between the couple and their in-laws, their friends and their community, have been the focus of repeated and intensive research. Perhaps no other area of sociology has received so much attention, and no other social group has been so thoroughly discussed in sociology textbooks.[1]

Can we say that the married parishioners among the friends of priests are more conservative and "settled" than the single parishioners? The available data of this survey allow us to test the assumption that marriage has a restrictive effect even on these very active and interested Catholics. We tested this hypothesis in a different culture, that of Santiago, Chile, where we asked many of these same questions, and found that married people were consistently more adaptive and ready for social change than were the single persons. We felt that the

decision to marry was in itself a symptom of adaptability and
that perhaps many of the single persons had not the courage
to take this important decision.[2]

On the other hand, sociological research has shown that religious observance decreases, especially among younger married persons, and that unmarried youths tend to go to Church
and to receive the sacraments with greater frequency.[3] If regularity of Church attendance is a correlate of conservatism,
there is a paradox here in decreased Church attendance and
increased conservatism.[4] Since all of the respondents to this
study are active parishioners, that is, frequent Church-goers,
we are not able at this point to explore this paradox.

Married and Single

There were more men than women among the friends of
priests who answered our questions, and the single people were,
on the average, younger than the married people. We are here
analyzing the effects of marital status, not the age factor, and
there is an obvious fallacy in comparing younger single persons
with older married persons. We matched the two categories
exactly for age, so that the average age of both single and
married is 36.2 years, with 57 percent of both below the age
of thirty-five years, and 11 percent of both at age fifty or
above. Since sex is presumed to be an important attitudinal
factor, we have matched the two groups so that exactly half of
each is male and half female.

Besides sex, age, and marital status, it is probable that education and economic status are influential in the attitudes of
parishioners. In the present comparison the single are somewhat better educated in the sense that more of them finished
their college education. The married parishioners, however, are

of a somewhat higher income status, although the great majority of both are in the middle income bracket. The differences between the single and the married are not great in these two variables; and since the tendencies are in opposite directions, they probably balance each other out.

TABLE 1—Comparative amount of schooling of married and single parishioners.

	(236) Married	(236) Single
High school incomplete	7%	7%
Completed high school	34	37
Some college	22	14
College graduate	37	42

TABLE 2—Comparative economic status of married and single respondents.

	(236) Married	(236) Single
Above average income	22%	15%
Middle income	71	75
Below average	7	10

These comparable groups of parishioners differ slightly also on the fact that more of the married (13%) than of the unmarried (8%) are converts to Catholicism. This appears to be a normal relationship between marriage and conversion to the Catholic religion. In a previous study we found that about three-quarters of the adult converts to the Church were attracted to Catholicism through engagement or marriage to a parishioner.[6] Interfaith marriage is often discussed from the negative point of view of "leakage" from the Church. The fact that there are more married male converts than females indicates that Catholic women bring their spouses into the Catholic

Church, while non-Catholic women probably bring their spouses out of the Catholic Church.[7]

The general question of marital differences with which we are here concerned can be discussed in a series of sub-hypotheses. These are questions which the data of this study allow us to test in a more or less orderly fashion. Are the married people more involved in religion and the Church than the single are? Do they have a better understanding of the priest's parish work, and a higher estimation of his priestly activities? Are the married persons more, or less, active than the single? Do they exhibit more conservative attitudes?

Church Involvement

Although married parishioners generally do not rate so high in religious observances, like Church-going and the reception of the sacraments, there are other norms against which their religious involvement may be measured. When we asked these parishioners whether their interest in important religious issues had increased during the past ten years, more of the married (58%) than of the single (43%) answered in the affirmative. This may suggest the assumption that religion becomes a more meaningful topic of interest and discussion among the married than among the single, even though this interest may not be expressed so much in external practices.[8]

From the point of view of periodical reading, however, the unmarried report a higher frequency of reading the only two Catholic journals that were on our check list. More of the single (35%) than of the married (27%) read *America,* and more of the single (31%) than of the married (17%) read the *Commonweal.* Two intervening factors may help to account for this difference. The single people read all periodicals, except *Saturday Evening Post* and *Reader's Digest,* more than the married do, which probably means that they have more time for reading. Secondly, the single have a somewhat higher average education than the married in this study; yet three-quarters of both categories say that they have great interest in reading for relaxation, and nine out of ten of both groups say that they read for information.

All of these respondents are active parishioners, and we have assumed throughout that involvement in Church affairs implies also fairly close relations with the clergy. Almost half of the married (48%), and a smaller proportion (41%) of the single report that the parish priest has been in their home several times, or often, during the past year. When we asked the purpose of these visits, we obtained a hint that the married are not only more friendly with the parish priest but also more involved in parochial activities. The priest paid a friendly social call more often to the married (29%) than to the single (20%). He also came more often on parish business to the married (20%) than to the single (13%).

We have no way of knowing how many of these single parishioners live by themselves in an apartment or rented room, a situation in which they are not so likely to entertain a priest as they would if they were living at home in a family. This difference of home environment, however, should not be an important factor in parishes where the priests regularly visit the parishioners, or take the yearly census.[9] The married people appear also to have more friends among the non-parochial clergy. More of the married (42%) than of the single (36%) said that they had entertained priests not of the parish as guests in their home several times, or often, during the past year.

The evidence at hand indicates that the married parishioners are more involved with religion and the Church than are the single persons. They are more interested in religious issues and they have closer contacts with the clergy. They do not read as often the two listed Catholic periodicals, but this does not seem significant enough to negate the affirmative conclusion to our hypothesis, tentative though it may be and open to further evidence.

Sympathy with Priest's Work

Do the married people have a higher appreciation of the work habits of the parish priest than the single people have? All of these unmarried respondents are gainfully employed, but for the most part this is true only of the husbands of the married couples. It is questionable to what extent this affects their judgment on the matter. In observing the efficiency of the priest, about four out of ten of both categories say that he gets his work done "without too much difficulty." Both of them also agree that the financial administration of the parish is the most time-consuming task of the priest. The married people rate the direction of parochial organizations, and the single rate the function of counselling, as the second most time-taking task of the priest.

TABLE 3—Judgment of occupational demands on priest, as compared to other professional men.

	(236) Married	(236) Single	(2183) Priests
Priest's are heavier	40%	52%	33%
About the same	42	35	32
Priest's are lighter	18	13	35

The single parishioners seem to have more sympathy with the work demands placed upon their priest, a larger proportion of them (52%) than of the married (40%) believing that the priest has to work harder than other professional men. The single are also more ready (51%) than the married (43%)— whose judgment must be based on personal experience—to say that the "worries" of the parish priest are greater than those of married men. The priests have a very different opinion of themselves on these two questions. Again, the single people are three times (31%) as likely as the married (10%) to say that the personal financial worries of the priest are greater than their own.[10]

TABLE 4—Judgment of the parish priest's worries, compared to those of most married men.

	(236)	(236)	(2183)
	Married	*Single*	*Priests*
Priest's are greater	43%	51%	18%
About the same	29	27	19
Priest's are less	27	22	62

Another area of opinion is that of the diocesan priest's personal financial status, about which most parishioners seem to have only a hazy notion. Occasionally one hears about a "rich priest," but few people realize how meager the salary is, and how limited the sources of income are, for the ordinary parish priest.[11] The sacerdotal vocation is obviously a non-profit occupation, yet it is assumed everywhere that the laborer is worthy of his hire. More than one-fifth of the diocesan parish priests (22%) report that they are in personal debt, and the same proportion (23%) say that they are approximately solvent. Only one out of ten of both the married and the single thinks that their parish priest friend is personally in debt.

TABLE 5—Comparison of parishioner's personal financial worries
with those of the parish priest.

	(236) Married	(236) Single
Priest's are heavier	10%	31%
About the same	30	31
Priest's are lighter	59	37

On the basis of these data, it is fairly clear that the married
parishioners are not quite so sympathetic to the hardships of
the priest's job as are the unmarried. Perhaps it is true that the
work, worry and responsibility of the married men are greater
—or seem greater to themselves—than those of either the
single layman or the parish priest. The priests themselves
apparently do not envy the lot of the married man, and they
are twice as likely as the laity to say that their work load is
lighter than that of other professional men.

We may here glance briefly at a few other opinions that the
parishioners have of their priests. For example, the single
people think that the priests spend much of their time in counselling parishioners, even though the priests themselves report
that unmarried adults take hardly any of their time.[12] Whether
or not marital status has an influence on this type of question,
more of the single (50%) than of the married (43%) feel
that the parish priest should have office hours like other professional men.

More than eight out of ten of both the married and the
single agree that the parish priests they know are favorable to
the participation of the laity in the liturgical functions of the
Church. There is also a fairly similar degree of accord—
although not so high—concerning their priest's interest in
encouraging young boys to enter the seminary. Approximately

two-thirds of both married and single parishioners say that the priests they know do promote vocations to the seminary.[13]

The friends of priests in general appear to have a high opinion of the sermons they hear during the year, only 5 percent of them saying that they consider these sermons poorly prepared. At the other pole of the range of opinion, however, there seems to be no logical explanation why more of the married (39%) than of the single (28%) think that these sermons are "extremely" well prepared. It is possible that parish priests generally point their sermons more at married people, at parents and family, than at unmarried adults, and that the former, therefore, find them of greater interest.

Social Awareness

The notion of settling down after marriage usually implies also that the attitudes of the married are more conservative than those of the single. For example, one of the social issues that is of vital concern to the liberal element in the American population is the question of basic civil rights for all people. The unmarried rate this of first importance, while the married rate it third, among the social goals worth striving for. The married people think that the reduction of crime and delinquency is of the greatest urgency. Aside from the norms of the liberal-conservative continuum, one would probably expect that married people, especially if they have children, would show a deeper concern about this kind of moral question.

If it can be assumed that Democratic political candidates, at least on the national scene, have a more liberal philosophy than their Republican opponents, it would appear that the majority of all the friends of priests are on the liberal side. The fact, however, that one-fourth of the married parishioners pre-

TABLE 6—Comparison by marital status of respondents' preference
        for national political candidates.

	(236) Married	(236) Single
Leaning toward Democrats	53%	54%
Toward Republicans	25	18
Independent voters	22	26

TABLE 7—Comparison by marital status of attitudes on the foreign
        economic aid program of the United States.

	(236) Married	(236) Single
Favor expanding it	41%	43%
Favor reducing it	35	31
Leave as it is	23	25

fer the Republican candidates may indicate a larger sprinkling
of conservatives among them than among the single.[14] The
question of foreign economic aid is also a favorite criterion by
which political liberals and conservatives can be measured,
but the present comparison by marital status shows practically
no difference of attitude.

We may explore further the question whether married
parishioners are less socially aware and active than single
parishioners. The usual assumption is that the married, by the
very nature of their commitment to spouse and family, do not
have time for social activities. The respondents themselves,
however, indicate that the answer depends largely upon the
kind of activity that is discussed. For example, a larger proportion of the married (55%) than of the single (46%) are
interested in following athletic contests and sports events.[15]
The implication seems to be that marriage and the family, with
the presence of growing children, involve parents more than
non-parents in athletic interests.

There was, however, a significant tendency in the opposite direction when we asked about their interests in "cultural" pursuits like music, art, and theater. A much larger proportion of the single (80%) than of the married (63%) say that they are now, or always have been interested in these kinds of activities. It is true that more of the married live in small-town parishes, and more of the single live in the large eastern dioceses, which may account for the differential availability of opportunities, yet the difference of interest appears to involve marital status as a decisive factor.

Other test questions may be used to probe social interest and activities. The problem of labor-management relations is one of these, and more of the married (51%) than of the single (43%) show increased interest in these problems. More married people (52%) than single people (31%) have become increasingly active in community organizations during the past decade. It is probable that deeper economic concerns have involved the married in questions of organized labor, and that the position of the family in the community has increased their involvement in civic organizations.

In drawing together these various segments of information, we must probably make the tentative conclusion that married people are more socially aware and active than single people. The statistical differences between the two categories are not great, but these findings may help to dispel the notion that people lessen their social awareness or withdraw into their conservative shell upon marriage.

Mixed Marriages

The expectation that Catholics who marry persons of other religions would differ noticeably from Catholics who marry fellow Catholics is not realized in the present study. The main reason seems to be that these are all "select" parishioners who are in this study because they are active, cooperative friends of the clergy. We do not conclude, of course, that the average mixed marriage works out the same way as the average Catholic marriage. All that we can say here is that the Catholic spouses in some interfaith marriages seem able to perform as excellent parishioners in spite of the supposed handicap of a non-Catholic partner.[16]

In order to compare these two types of marriage, we again matched them and equalized the factors of sex and age. The expected regional disparities appear in this comparison, with the rate of mixed marriages lowest in the areas where the Catholic population is most numerous. About the same proportion of both (46%) attended public high school for four years, and the same proportion (23%) of both finished college. One difference, however, shows up in the amount of parental education. More of the spouses in mixed marriages had parents who attended college than is the case of those who married Catholics.

Since the marriage in which both spouses are Catholics has twice as much opportunity for contacting the clergy as the marriage with only one Catholic spouse, we may expect that the former has more clerical visitors to the home. The parish priest, however, does not seem to show any preference in this regard since he appears to visit both types of home with about the same frequency. The difference in the circle of priestly friendships is seen in the fact that more of the Catholic marriages (44%) than of the mixed (28%) report that a non-parochial priest has been a guest in the home several times, or often, during the past year.

There is apparently an influence of the non-Catholic spouse —in most cases, a husband—in areas of thinking and behavior which are not strictly religious. For example, more of the persons in mixed marriages (30%) than in Catholic marriages (21%) are Republicans in national politics. They are also more interested (91%) than the others (82%) in the problem of race relations. There is also a difference in the fact that they think the securing of civil rights is the most important social goal of the American people, while those in Catholic marriages feel that the reduction of crime and delinquency is of paramount importance.

TABLE 8—Comparative frequency of reading three non-sectarian periodicals.

	(136) Mixed Marriages	(272) Catholic Marriages
Time	77%	69%
Harper's Magazine	38	21
Atlantic Monthly	24	13

When we asked them about the frequency with which they read certain selected periodicals, we found that both categories of respondents read the two Catholic magazines, *America* and *Commonweal,* in about the same proportions. But Table 8 shows that there is a significant difference in the frequency of reading certain non-sectarian periodicals. It seems that the non-Catholic spouse opens up a larger area of reading interest, and in this respect the mixed marriage has an advantage over the marriage between two Catholics. A social and intellectual stimulus is provided for wider horizons of interest.

Summary

In attempting to summarize these various comparisons and hypotheses, we realize that all of these parishioners display a kind of exemplary Catholicism. From this point of view most of the comparative categories are already fairly well "matched" so that differences are of relative degree rather than of extreme poles. Nevertheless, marriage, and the kind of marriage, does make a difference in the Church life of the individual.

1. Although not as regular in Church attendance as the single parishioners, the married are somewhat closer to the Church and the priests than are the single.[17] They seem to develop more interest in religious issues after marriage.

2. Priests must be assumed to have the surest judgment on their own parochial work and worries. From this point of view, the married people are closer to the priests' own appraisal, but the single seem to show a more sympathetic understanding of the parish priest's role.

3. The assumption that married persons are more conservative than single persons seems to rest on a common comparison between young unmarried people with older married people. When age levels are held constant, as in the present study, this expected tendency toward conservatism does not show up among the married. It appears, indeed, that the married are somewhat more progressive and socially aware than the single.

4. The friends of priests who are in interfaith marriages have as much contact with the parish priest as do the other parishioners, but do not have nearly as much contact with non-parochial priests. This may indicate that they focus their religious activities and friendships on the parish level.

5. On the other hand, Catholics in mixed marriages seem to be more alert to the broader issues of society, and to have a greater spread of moral and intellectual interests, than do the parishioners who are married to Catholics.

NOTES

1. For some studies of marriage and the family by Catholic sociologists, see Frances Wood, *The American Family System* (New York: Harper Brothers, 1959); John L. Thomas, *The American Catholic Family* (Englewood Cliffs: Prentice-Hall, 1956); and Lucius Cervantes, in Carle C. Zimmerman and Lucius Cervantes, *Marriage and the Family* (Chicago: Regnery, 1956).

2. This is a conclusion we reached in the research study reported in *Cambio Social en Chile*, ch. 7, "Casados y Solteros."

3. See the summary of research data in Michael Argyle, *Religious Behaviour* (Glencoe: Free Press, 1958), and the later findings on Catholics in Joseph Schuyler, *Northern Parish* (Chicago: Loyola University Press, 1960), pp. 222f.

4. These terms, conservatism and liberalism, must be used with great caution when dealing with religious and theological questions. See, for example, Willard A. Kerr, "Untangling the Liberalism-Conservatism Continuum," *Journal of Social Psychology*, vol. 35 (February, 1952), pp. 111-125.

5. For differences in religious practices by age, sex, and marital status, see Fichter, *Social Relations in the Urban Parish*, ch. 7, "The Religious Life-Profile."

6. Fichter, *Southern Parish* (Chicago: University of Chicago Press, 1951), p. 40. For a bibliography on interfaith marriages, see Paul H. Besanceney, "Unbroken Protestant-Catholic Marriages among Whites in the Detroit Area," *The American Catholic Sociological Review*, vol. 23, no. 1 (Spring, 1962), pp. 3-20; also Albert I. Gordon, *Intermarriage: Interfaith, Interracial, Interethnic* (Boston: Beacon Press, 1964). For a popular Protestant presentation, see James A. Pike, *If You Marry Outside Your Faith* (New York: Harper Brothers, 1954).

7. There is no logical reason why Catholic women are attracted to non-Catholic men more than Catholic men are attracted to non-Catholic women, yet the statistics on valid Catholic marriages have long indicated this disparity. The hunch that Catholic men marry outside the Church invalidly more than Catholic women do seems

to be confirmed in the careful research by Lee Burchinal, William Kenkel, and Loren Chancellor, "Comparisons of State- and Diocese-Reported Marriage Data, 1953-57," *The American Catholic Sociological Review,* vol. 23, no. 1 (Spring, 1962), pp. 21-29.

8. In an earlier study, Gerhard Lenski, "Social Correlates of Religious Interest," *American Sociological Review,* vol. 18, no. 5 (October, 1953), pp. 533-544, found that couples with children had significantly more interest in religion than the childless couples, but he also indicates that the latter were "childless by choice, not by necessity."

9. Twenty-two percent of all parishioners said that the parish census had been taken within the year, and more than six out of ten said it had been taken within the last three years.

10. We did not ask the priests to compare their own financial status with that of the laity. Income, as a criterion of status and success, presents a peculiar problem in the study of religious functionaries. See the discussion in Fichter, *Religion as an Occupation,* pp. 176-180.

11. A middle-aged, married businessman with above average income thinks his pastor friend has a higher standard of living than his because "he drives a Cadillac—we drive a Ford."

12. The priests report that school children take up most of their time, married people are next, and teenagers are third.

13. It may be surmised that parents are more aware of this kind of vocation promotion, since it may affect their children, but the responses do not support this assumption. A survey in 1964 of 8,689 parents in the Peoria Diocese showed them quite unsure about the parental role in promoting vocation: forty-one percent would actively encourage it, thirty-one percent would discuss it only if the child brought up the question, the rest would pray and leave the matter in God's hands.

14. Since these two categories are matched for sex and age, and are fairly similar in education and income, the preference for political party is not so clear-cut as a function of marital status. As an example of the kind of studies made about factors in voting, see Seymour M. Lipset, *Political Man* (Garden City: Doubleday,

1959); also Bernard Berelson, Paul Lazersfeld, William McPhee, *Voting* (Chicago: University of Chicago Press, 1954).

15. The notion that the parish priest is preoccupied with athletics, and "reads the sports page first" in the newspaper, may be re-examined in the light of the following comparison.

TABLE 9—Extent to which interest has increased or decreased in sports.

	(2183) Priests	(1275) Laymen
Always was interested	31%	43%
Now more interested	11	10
Never was interested	23	19
Now less interested	35	28

16. In an unpublished nation-wide study of Catholic young men in military service, we found that the religious observance of the parent had a more important influence on the son than the fact whether the parents were in a mixed or Catholic marriage.

17. Yet the single persons seem to be closer to the bishop of their diocese, more of them (35%) than of the married (19%) having met or known him personally.

CHAPTER SIX

Older and Younger Parishioners

The study of behavioral and attitudinal differences between younger and older people is the stock in trade of the sociologist. Inter-generational conflict is often the theme, not only of the novelist and playwright, but also of the careful social scientist.[1] Youth is a significant cultural value in American society, and it is only in recent years, and as a consequence of increased longevity, that some attention is being paid to the aging.[2] The emphasis is still on youth, however, and relatively little scientific research has been done concerning the function of religion among our aging citizens.[3]

The notion that there is wisdom in old age, and that there is "nothing like experience," is the kind of common sense statement that is usually accepted without question. The assumption too is widespread, that oldsters become conservative and that social change and innovation are the business of young people. In the present study of Catholic parishioners we are able to derive some of the differences that exist between the older and the younger generation, and in some instances to compare them with the differences by age categories among the priests with whom they are friendly.

TABLE 1—Comparative age categories of parishioners and of parish priests.

	(2216) *Laity*	(2183) *Priests*
25-29 years	11%	18%
30-39	36	33
40-49	32	28
50-59	14	15
60 years and older	7	6

The principal comparisons here will be made between the youngest lay persons, 25-29 years of age, who number 246 parishioners, and the oldest category, sixty years of age and older, who number 153 persons. The matching age groupings among the parish priests contain 404 in the younger clergy and 129 in the older.

Background Differences

Besides the factor of age, certain other variables differ expectedly between the older and the younger friends of priests. For example, the youngest parishioners tend more to be in the middle income bracket, while the oldest have a greater spread of income, with more persons at both above-average and below-average levels. There are more women in the youngest group and more men in the oldest.

TABLE 2—Age comparison of income status among the parishioners.

	(246) *Youngest*	(153) *Oldest*
Above average income	19%	25%
Middle income	71	61
Below average	10	14

TABLE 3—Age comparison of marital status of parishioners.

	(246) Youngest	(153) Oldest
Never married	38%	16%
Married now	61	65
Widowed or separated	1	19

TABLE 4—Age comparison of Catholic and mixed marriages of those who have ever been married.

	(152) Youngest	(129) Oldest
Married to Catholic	95	81
Married to non-Catholic	5	19

Obviously the younger parishioners contain a larger proportion of unmarried persons, and the older people are more likely to have been widowed. This fact should not distort our findings, however, since we have already seen that difference in marital status is not nearly so influential as difference in age.[4] One of the interesting aspects of marital status among these nuclear parishioners is that the oldsters are four times as likely as the youngsters to have contracted a marriage with a non-Catholic spouse. Whether or not this indicates a trend toward fewer mixed marriages among the younger friends of priests

TABLE 5—Age and sex distribution of marriages in which both spouses are Catholics.

	(1157) Males	(627) Females	(1884) Total
25-29 years	97.5%	91.5%	94.7%
30-39	98.8	88.1	94.9
40-49	97.2	76.4	93.1
50-59	96.8	76.8	88.0
60 years and older	94.2	74.4	87.6

is still an open question, although the statistics for this total study indicate that this is the case among the married females.

The two polar age categories in this comparison differ also in the amount and kind of education they have had. Half of the younger parishioners had four years of Catholic high school, and 40 percent of them had four years of public high school. Among the older people, however, there was much less Catholic schooling, one-fifth (19%) of them having had a full four years of Catholic high school, while three out of ten (31%) had four years of public high school.

The contrast in the amount of schooling is sharpened when we realize that two out of five older parishioners did not attend, or did not finish, high school, while two out of five of the young generation are college graduates.[5] This generational difference reflects not only the increasing educational attainments of American Catholics, but also the generally raised levels of schooling in the total American population.[6] Among the younger people eight out of ten of their fathers, and a higher proportion (86%) of their mothers, never attended college. Among the parents of older parishioners non-attendance at college is 91 percent for fathers and 95 percent for mothers.

TABLE 6—Age comparison of the amount of schooling completed by parishioners.

	(246) Youngest	(153) Oldest
High school incomplete	4%	41%
High school graduate	35	21
Some college	20	19
College graduate	41	19

In formulating hypotheses to test the age differentials among these lay friends of priests, we must keep this factor of education in mind. As we have seen, the amount of schooling is often a significant factor in the formation of social attitudes, so that it may be debatable in this context whether older persons think the way they do because of their advanced age, or because they have had less formal education.[7]

Our central theme concerns the attitudes and relations of parishioners to their clergy and the Church. The information we have gathered allows us, therefore, to test certain hypotheses dealing with age differences. Do the older people have closer and more intimate relations with the parish priests? Are the younger parishioners more critical, or less appreciative, of the clergy? Are the older people more critical of their fellow parishioners? Are the younger persons more progressive and socially alert than the older?

Clergy-Lay Relations

The mere fact that the older parishioners have lived longer, and have had the opportunity to become acquainted with more priests during their lifetime, would lead to the assumption that they have closer relations with the clergy. This expectation is realized in the fact that four out of ten of the older generation have personally met the bishop of their diocese, while only one-fourth of the younger parishioners could make this claim. Although all of these parishioners are active and interested in the Church, only one-tenth (9%) of the older persons, and one-fifth of the younger (19%) have ever even *seen* their bishop.

One of the measures of personal relations is the frequency with which people visit one another's homes. In this respect, we find that the priest pays more attention to his older parishioners, half of whom say that the parish priest has been in

TABLE 7—Age comparison of frequency of home visits by parish
priests in past year.

	(246) Youngest	(153) Oldest
Not at all	46%	34%
Only once	16	16
Several times	21	31
Often	17	19

their home several times or often during the past year. Less
than two out of five (38%) of the younger parishioners make
this statement. In about one-fourth of the cases the purpose
of the priestly visit was a friendly social call for both the
young and the old. As may be expected, however, the oldsters
are almost four times as likely (15%) as the youngsters (4%)
to say that the parish priest came to them because of sickness
in the family.

TABLE 8—Age comparison of frequency of home visits by non-
parish priests in past year.

	(246) Youngest	(153) Oldest
Not at all	48%	36%
Only once	13	11
Several times	28	31
Often	11	22

We find also that the older people tend more often to have
priest guests from outside their parish than do the younger persons. More than half of them (53%), as compared to four out
of ten (39%) of the younger parishioners, had a non-parish
priest in their home several times or often during the year. In
this regard there are probably other explanatory factors, be-

sides the longer life and the wider acquaintanceship of the older parishioners. As we have seen, they are slightly better off financially, and can probably afford to do more entertaining. They are also free of the inconvenience of having small children in the home, a fact which sometimes makes it difficult for younger married people to entertain guests.[8]

We have no way of knowing presently whether younger priests visit younger parishioners, while the older pastors visit mainly the older folks in the parish. On the criterion of the priest's visits to the homes of lay people, the data of this study show quite clearly that the older parishioners have more frequent contact and closer personal relations with the parish clergy than do the younger people.

Estimation of Parish Clergy

A second hypothesis we may deal with here is the question whether younger parishioners are more likely to be critical of the clergy than the oldsters are. It is generally assumed that young Catholics are more impatient for change and improvement, more critical of the status quo, less satisfied with traditional patterns of thought and behavior. On several of the items usable in this area, we can also seek out the age distinctions among the parish priests themselves. There is almost always a clear-cut difference among the clergy, but often the opinions and attitudes of the younger priests are closer to those of the older parishioners.[9]

One indication of this generational difference of opinion is that the youngest parishioners are less willing (37%) than the oldest (48%) to approve the traditional pattern whereby a boy starts his studies for the priesthood in the minor seminary at the age of thirteen years.[10] This difference of opinion may

TABLE 9—Age comparison of clergy and laity who are in favor of
sending 13-year old boy to minor seminary.

(246)	Younger laity	37%
(153)	Older laity	48
(404)	Younger clergy	49
(129)	Older clergy	57

be partly due to the influence of priest friends. Table 9 gives
the answers of the parish priests themselves; but three-quarters
(77%) of the older parishioners, and six out of ten (61%)
of the younger, say that the priest they know best greatly encourages boys to enter the seminary.

TABLE 10—Age comparison of clergy and laity who say that
parish priests favor lay participation in the liturgy.

(246)	Younger laity	83%
(153)	Older laity	74
(404)	Younger clergy	73
(129)	Older clergy	43

If the priest friends of the younger generation do not work
quite so hard in encouraging vocations to the seminary, they
do indeed seem to give more encouragement to the participation of the laity in the liturgy of the Church. This difference
is reflected even more significantly in the opinion of younger
priests about their contemporaries and the older priests about

TABLE 11—Age comparison of clergy and laity who say that
sermons are very well prepared.

(246)	Younger laity	28%
(153)	Older laity	50
(404)	Younger clergy	29
(129)	Older clergy	15

theirs. Lay participation in the liturgy is evidently still a young movement among Catholics in the United States.

There is a reversal of this attitude on the question of the sermons that the parishioners have heard. The younger people seem to be much more critical of pulpit efforts in the parish; less than three out of ten of them, as compared to half of the older persons, say that the sermons are very well prepared. When we asked the priests the facts about their own sermon preparation, we found that twice as many of the younger clergy as of the older prepare their preaching very well in the sense that they write out the complete sermon.[11]

In most of these questions we asked the parishioner to make an appraisal of the priest he knows best, and there is a strong indication in their responses that the younger laity are talking about the younger clergy, while the older laity are talking about the older clergy. This surmise emerges from the fact that the older parishioners are twice as likely (72%) as the younger (36%) to say that the priest they know best is the pastor of the parish. No demonstration is required to prove that among the diocesan clergy pastors are always older than their curates.[12]

TABLE 12—Age comparison of clergy and laity who say that the parish priest works harder than other professionals.

(246)	Younger laity	51%
(153)	Older laity	40
(404)	Younger clergy	40
(129)	Older clergy	26

When we asked our respondents to compare the work demands made on parish priests with those made on other professional men, we found a significant difference between the laity and the clergy, as well as between the polar age categories of both. Perhaps the elderly priest friends of the older lay people do not actually work so hard as the youthful priest friends of the younger generation. The parish priests are here undoubtedly reflecting their own experience at work, as well as the knowledge they have of other professional men.[13] It is to be expected that professional men in their sixties begin to relax their work activities, but perhaps not more so than priests in their sixties.

From this point of view it appears that the older parishioners are more critical of the clergy, although there is always the question whether the friends of priests really know what the work demands are on the parish priest. We asked our respondents further to compare the "worries" of the parish priest with those of married men. An odd reversal of opinion occurs here. The younger parishioners, of whom fewer are married, are a little less willing (47%) than the older generation (53%) to say that the parish priest's worries are heavier than those of married men.[14] On the other hand, more of the younger priests than of the older make this same appraisal, although the estimates of both are much more modest than those of the laity.

One curious disparity arises in response to the question whether pastors, as distinguished from curates, should be peri-

TABLE 13—Age comparison of clergy and laity who think the worries of the parish priest are heavier than those of married men.

(246)	Younger laity	47%
(153)	Older laity	53
(404)	Younger clergy	22
(129)	Older clergy	16

odically transferred from one parish to another. A larger proportion of the younger people (76%) than of the older (67%) prefer that the pastor should remain permanently in the same parish. While the difference of opinion is not so great in relation to the transfer of the curate, a smaller proportion (51%) of the younger generation than of the older (55%) prefer parochial stability for the assistant parish priest.

The data that we are using here to test this hypothesis seem to be of unequal weight. Are the younger parishioners more critical of the priests? They do not think so much of the sermons they hear, but they are almost as concerned as the older parishioners about the worries that the priest endures. On the other hand, they have a higher appreciation of the work load of the priest, and of the favorable attitude of the clergy toward lay participation in the liturgy. We must probably say then that the younger parishioners have a higher estimation of the parish clergy than do the older parishioners.

Estimation of the Laity

Does age make a difference in the way that the friends of priests look at their fellow parishioners? Are the young people more likely to be critical of their fellow laymen in parochial and civic organizations? It is a fairly common complaint of our informants who live in long-established parishes that the lay groups are largely in the hands of an entrenched "old guard." In sociological studies of parish life we have seen why this kind of situation develops. It is one of the inherent organizational problems of getting fuller participation by the largest number of parishioners in the lay groups of the Church.[15] In the present study we find that the younger respondents are more likely (65%) than the older (57%) to be active and interested in lay and civic groups.[16] These are not normal percentages in the ordinary parish because these friends of priests are selected parishioners.

TABLE 14—Age comparison of clergy and laity who think that adult parishioners are cooperative in important projects.

(246)	Younger laity	78%
(153)	Older laity	88
(404)	Younger clergy	75
(129)	Older clergy	86

Generally speaking, both clergy and laity have a fairly high regard for the spirit of cooperation among the adult parishioners when there is an important parochial project under way. In this instance, there is a remarkable similarity in the proportion of responses of the priests and the people, but the age differential shows up again in both categories. The older people, both lay and clerical, are more likely than the younger to have a favorable estimation of the parishioners. While the differences are not great they suggest that the older generation is less critical of the laity.

TABLE 15—Age comparison of clergy and laity who say that officers and leaders of parish groups have initiative and a sense of responsibility.

		Initiative	*Responsibility*
(246)	Younger laity	54%	82%
(153)	Older laity	52	80
(404)	Younger clergy	43	82
(129)	Older clergy	42	71

Voluntary groups, of the kind found in every Catholic parish, depend heavily on the initiative and responsibility of their lay officers. The priests, both young and old, tend to have a lower opinion than the laity does about the spirit of initiative demonstrated by the officers and leaders of parish groups. In many parishes this problem centers around the areas of activities in which it is possible for the laity to use their initiative. Even where the areas are defined, it is still up to the pastor to allow and encourage lay initiative.

When we speak of lay responsibility in parish groups, we must probably include those programs in which the priests have taken the initiative but expect the parishioners to have the responsibility in carrying it through. Here we find that the parishioners, both young and old, are in agreement with the younger priests. The older clergy, however, has a lower opinion of lay responsibility. Perhaps they are more accustomed to doing things themselves rather than depending upon the lay people.

TABLE 16—Age comparison of lay opinion on position priest should take in parish societies.

	(246) Younger	(153) Older
Equal vote with lay members	18%	16%
Advice and counsel only	59	51
Power of veto, final decision	20	23
Complete control	3	10

In a subtle question concerning the preferable position of the priest in parochial lay organizations, we find that the older lay persons have a tendency to depend upon the clergy. The differences are not significant, but it seems worth noting that three times more of the older generation (10%) than of the younger (3%) are willing to give over complete control of lay groups to the parish priest.[17]

The data presented here are probably not precise enough, nor the differences large enough, to allow a positive conclusion to the hypothesis that younger parishioners are more critical of the laity than older parishioners are. The younger people are not so high in their praise of their fellow parishioners' cooperation, have about the same opinion about the initiative and responsibility of lay leaders, and are a little more reluctant to allow the priest veto power and complete control of the lay groups in the parish.

Progressive Parishioners

The final sub-hypothesis that we might discuss here is the generally accepted assumption that younger people express the more progressive ideas, and older people the more traditional ones. Several items in this study give fairly conclusive confirmation to this hypothesis, for both the priests and their lay friends.

American liberals are concerned about civil rights, and we find here that our youngest informants consider the securing of basic citizen rights, regardless of race or creed, as the most important social goal toward which the American people should strive. They think that the reduction of cold war tensions is second in importance, and the reduction of crime and delinquency is third. The older people also believe that these are the most urgent social goals to be achieved, but they put the problems of crime and delinquency in first place, the basic rights of citizens in second, and the tensions of the cold war in third.

Perhaps the most reliable contemporary test to distinguish liberal from traditional tendencies is one's attitude toward the foreign economic aid program of the United States. Conserv-

TABLE 17—Age comparison of clergy and laity on attitude toward the foreign economic aid program.

	Laity		Priests	
	(246)	(153)	(404)	(129)
	Younger	*Older*	*Younger*	*Older*
Favor expanding it	44%	30%	53%	28%
Favor reducing it	30	38	22	38
Leave as it is	26	30	21	31

atives and traditionalists often deplore America's foreign "entanglements," while liberals feel that foreign aid is one of America's moral responsibilities. In the present study only a minority of all four categories would be in favor of reducing this program, and this minority is larger among the older laity and clergy. The younger priests have an even larger proportion (53%) than the younger lay people (44%) who are in favor of expanding the program.

It seems useful also to employ another index of liberal and conservative attitudes in the form of stated preferences for national political candidates. A clear-cut age differential appears here, with a larger proportion of the younger generation, both priests and lay persons, choosing the Democrats over the Republicans.

TABLE 18—Age comparison of clergy and laity on preferences for national political candidates.

	Laity		Priests	
	(246)	(153)	(404)	(129)
	Younger	*Older*	*Younger*	*Older*
Prefer Democrats	52%	47%	46%	34%
Prefer Republicans	20	27	16	20
Independent voters	26	25	34	40

Various kinds of social problems lend themselves as norms for the measurement of progressive and traditional attitudes. Usually, people who take an interest in international affairs, race relations, and labor problems, are considered social-minded and progressive. Of course, one may take a deeply negative attitude toward these questions, as is customary among so-called conservatives. What our data show is that for the most part, the younger respondents, both clergy and lay, express more interest than the older people in these problems. There is also a consistently greater interest at all age levels on the part of the parishioners than there is on the part of the parish priests.

TABLE 19—Age comparison of clergy and laity who are interested in three social problems.

	Laity		Priests	
	(246)	(153)	(404)	(129)
	Younger	*Older*	*Younger*	*Older*
International affairs	96%	88%	80%	63%
Race relations	89	76	76	53
Labor problems	65	68	60	51

It is probable that people change their interests as they grow older and that they focus their attention on different areas of interest.[18] In the present study there are exceptions to this generalization. For example, almost all (96%) of the parishioners, both young and old, profess continued interest in religious issues. This may be expected from this select nucleus of faithful Catholics. There is an age similarity present also, but at a much lower proportion, in the area of athletics and sports events. About half (52%) of both young and old parishioners say they are interested in following sports, while among the priests, fewer of the older men (33%) than of the younger (54%) express an interest in athletics and sports.

This final sub-hypothesis tests out positively, that is, it shows quite clearly that younger people are socially alert, more liberal and progressive than older people. They consider civil rights the foremost American social goal to be achieved. They are more in favor of expanding the foreign economic aid program. They are more likely to be in favor of Democratic candidates, and are also more interested in vital social issues.

Summary

We have been comparing one set of people in their late twenties with another set who are mainly in their sixties. It is almost like comparing grandchildren with grandparents since these respondents are separated by a whole generation. Some variables, like education, marital and economic status, have not been controlled, but it may be assumed in this case that their different influences balance each other out. The inter-generational differences tend to follow our expectations, and may be briefly summarized here.

1. The older parishioners have more friends among the clergy, and have more frequent personal contact both with parish priests and with priests who are doing non-parochial work.

2. In general, the younger parishioners seem to have a better understanding and appreciation of the work of the parish priest. Age differences show up here also among the clergy, with the younger priests being more realistic than the older.

3. There is a tendency on the part of the younger people to be more critical of their fellow parishioners, but the difference of attitude here does not appear to be significant.

4. No doubt exists about the more progressive and liberal attitudes of the younger respondents, both clergy and laity. By every important criterion of measurement, the older generation shows itself more conservative.

5. Other sections of this report indicate clergy-laity similarities and contrasts. While the priests in most instances are more conservative than the parishioners, the younger priests differ considerably from the older in this respect.

NOTES

1. The paper by Kingsley Davis, "The Sociology of Parent-Youth Conflict," *American Sociological Review*, vol. 5, no. 4 (August, 1940), pp. 523-535, is probably still a valid analysis of intergenerational differences.
2. Clark Tibbitts and Wilma Donahue (eds.), *Aging in Today's Society* (Englewood Cliffs: Prentice-Hall, 1960) contains numerous readings and a useful bibliography on the subject.
3. The Report of the White House Conference on Aging, *The Nation and Its Older People* (Washington, D.C.: Government Printing Office, 1961), contains only four pages on the relation of religion to old age. Two books, indicating the concern of Protestants about this question, are by Paul B. Maves and J. Lennart Cedarleaf, *Older People and the Church* (Nashville: Abingdon-Cokesbury, 1949), and Virginia Stafford, *Older Adults in the Church* (New York: Methodist Publishing House, 1953).
4. See the discussion above, ch. 5, "Marriage and Settling Down."
5. See the findings on schooling above, ch. 2, "The College Graduate."
6. Generalizations about the educational comparison between Catholics and non-Catholics must be made cautiously from these data because these friends of priests represent above-average educational attainment. For the total population figures, see U. S. Bureau of the Census, "Projections of Educational Attainment in the

United States, 1960 to 1980," *Current Population Reports,* Series
P-20, no. 91 (1959).
7. The measurement of conservatism with increasing age presents
the inherent problems of the longitudinal study. Do the individuals themselves change as they grow older, or do they only
seem to become more conservative in comparison to the younger
generation which is living in the midst of more liberal ideas?
8. Priests are probably more likely to visit the homes of married
people, but this does not affect the age comparisons here since
the proportion (38%) of single persons in the youngest age
bracket is almost matched by the combined proportion (35%) of
the oldsters who are either single (16%) or widowed (19%).
9. This appears to be another aspect of the "lag" between Catholic
laity and clergy, noted by Daniel Callahan, *The Mind of the
Catholic Layman,* p. 130, and discussed earlier in Fichter, *Religion
as an Occupation,* p. 87.
10. In our survey of 1,287 Catholic parents in New Orleans we found
25 percent who would allow their son to enter the minor seminary
upon graduation from elementary school. In the Peoria Survey of
8,689 Catholic parents, this proportion of approval declined to 16
percent.
11. This comparison is not necessarily invidious. Older priests frequently preserve a "backlog" of sermons that they have written
earlier in their career.
12. Among the younger priests, under thirty years of age, only two
percent are pastors, as compared to more than ninety percent of
the priests who are sixty years of age or older.
13. Opinions of the work demands of various professions seem to
grow out of the "images" created about occupations, even at the
training level. For example, only sixteen percent of 545 major
seminarians in a religious congregation feel that they have to
study harder than students preparing for other professions; yet,
six out of ten (59%) of 348 diocesan minor seminarians feel that
they have to study harder than young men of their own age who
are not preparing for the priesthood.
14. When the categories of married and single parishioners are
matched for sex and age (as we have seen above in chapter 5)

more of the single (51%) than of the married (43%) think that the parish priest's worries are greater than those of married men.

15. See Fichter, *Social Relations in the Urban Parish,* ch. 12, "The Structure of Parochial Societies," and also *Parochial School,* ch. 17, "School, Parish and Community." For some cross-denominational comparisons, see David Moberg, *The Church as a Social Institution,* under the heading, "Lay Leadership in the Church," pp. 414-418.

16. This age difference is found also among the clergy, the corresponding proportions being 59 percent for the younger priests and 36 percent for the older priests.

17. This same question was used in a study of social change in Santiago, Chile, where we found a significantly higher percentage of both young and old who wanted the parish priest to have only an equal vote with the laity.

	(116) Youngest	(79) Oldest
Equal vote with lay members	33%	27%
Advice and counsel only	62	59
Power of veto, final decision	4	6
Complete control	1	8

18. See the discussion on "adjustment" in old age by Robert M. Gray and David O. Moberg, *The Church and the Older Person* (Grand Rapids: Eerdmans, 1962). Certain religious beliefs, as in the existence of God and the after-life, seem to grow stronger as people get older. For research data on this matter, see Michael Argyle, *Religious Behaviour* (Glencoe: Free Press, 1959), pp. 67-69.

CHAPTER SEVEN

Convert Parishioners

One of the areas of American Catholic life about which we have very little scientific information is that of converts to the Catholic Church.[1] Techniques have been carefully worked out for attracting people to the Catholic religion; advertisements are placed in popular magazines; convert courses are presented in many parishes and schools. Every parish priest gives convert instructions, either to individuals or groups, and keeps careful records of adult baptisms. With the growth of the American population, there is also an annual increase in the numbers of converts, as recorded in the *Catholic Directory*.[2]

What happens to converts after they come into the parish?[3] Assumptions are widely made that "converts make the best Catholics." They are said to put born Catholics "to shame" by their religious zeal and knowledge. The accepted notion is that they have "thought their way" into the Church, and must therefore have a much more intelligent basis for their beliefs. A young news reporter among the friends of priests says, "as a convert I think I can safely say I know more about the faith than most Catholics who were baptized as infants." There are undoubtedly many outstanding examples of active, dedi-

cated converts. We have found them in previous studies, but
we have also found nominal and dormant parishioners among
the converts.[4]

Who Are the Converts?

The respondents to this nation-wide study of parishioners
were selected because they are active, Church-going people.
Both converts and non-converts among them attend religious
services regularly. The proportion of converts among our informants is highest in the South Central States, the Southwest,
and on the Pacific Coast. It is lowest in New England and the
East. This is obviously a function of the population distribution of Catholics in the United States. Where the Catholic
concentration is largest the rate of conversions is lowest, and
vice versa.

According to our data, the sex ratio of converts favors the
females, but the difference is not so great as is ordinarily supposed. Of the female respondents to this study, 13 percent
are converts, as compared to 11 percent of the males. Almost
six out of ten (59%) of the men came into the Church during
their twenties, but the sex distribution at age of entrance into
the Church is quite similar.

TABLE 1—Sex comparison of convert's age at entrance to Church.

	(145) Males	(127) Females	(272) Total
Under 20 years of age	13%	17%	15%
20-24 years	34	33	33
25-29	25	18	22
30-34	9	11	10
35-44	10	12	11
45 years and older	9	9	9

The age at which people decide to become Catholics appears to be related with their marital status. Sociological studies indicate that the single largest channel of conversion to Catholicism is mixed marriage.[5] More non-Catholic males than females come into the Church by this route, and since most marriages occur when the spouses are in their twenties, this probably accounts for the larger proportion of male converts in this age bracket.[6] It is also an interesting aspect of this marital phenomenon that larger proportions of female converts are still single, or are married to non-Catholics, than is the case for the males.

TABLE 2—Sex comparison of marital status of non-converts and of converts.

	Non-converts		Converts	
	(1130)	(814)	(145)	(127)
	Males	*Females*	*Males*	*Females*
Never married	10%	25%	6%	10%
Married to Catholic	87	62	93	82
Married to non-Catholic	3	13	1	8

Social Status of Converts

One of the hypotheses we may test here concerns the status differential between converts and non-converts. Do the priests seek out people of higher social status to convert them to the Church? Is Catholicism more attractive to one social class than to another? From our data we can obtain some small hints that may help to answer these questions. We are dealing only with active Catholics and not with a representative sample of the total adult Catholic population. Furthermore, the only usable criteria of status available to us are occupation and levels of education and income.

The amount of education of parents is indicative of the social class of the family to which respondents belong. In this respect we find no difference between the converts and the non-converts. One out of eight (13%) of the fathers, and one out of ten (9%) of the mothers, of both attended or finished college. Half of the converts (51%) and slightly more of the non-converts (55%) attended or finished college.

TABLE 3—Comparative amount of schooling finished by converts and non-converts.

	(1944) Non-converts	(272) Converts
High school incomplete	14%	19%
High school graduate	31	30
Some college	20	20
College graduate	35	31

The differences in the amount of education do not appear significant, but to the extent that they do exist they indicate that the average years of schooling of converts are somewhat less than those of non-converts. An obvious and expected datum is the fact that converts are much less likely (5%) than the non-converts (45%) to have attended a Catholic high school.

This slight education differential is balanced in the other direction in the comparison of income status. The converts include a slightly higher proportion (31%) than the non-converts do (26%) of respondents who say that their income is above average. This minor difference is borne out also when we asked these people to compare their material standard of living with that of the priest they know best.

TABLE 4—Comparative income status of converts and non-converts.

	(1944) Non-converts	(272) Converts
Above average income	26%	31%
Middle income	66	61
Below average	8	8

TABLE 5—Estimation of own standard of living compared with that of priest friend.

	(1944) Non-converts	(272) Converts
Mine is higher	22%	25%
About the same	54	54
Mine is lower	23	20

The amount of education and the level of income are closely related to the type of occupation or profession that people have. Since the two criteria of education and income are quite similar between the converts and the non-converts, the fact is that there is no significant difference in their occupational categories. Both groups have the same representation in the same range of occupation. On the basis of these data, therefore, it appears that converts are of about the same social status as other Catholics. These findings may be indicative of a much broader generalization to the effect that status-wise the American Catholic population now reflects fairly accurately the total American white population.[7]

This seems to be another way of saying that the conversion process, as reflected among the friends of priests, is selective only in the sense that typical Americans become Catholics. Since the Church embraces all social strata within its membership, it also receives converts at all social levels.[8] Unlike some Protestant denominations, Catholicism cannot be termed either a "class" religion or a "mass" religion.

Priest-Convert Relations

Are converts likely to have closer personal relations with the parish priests and other clergy than non-converts have? The hypothesis may be advanced that the adult experience of taking instructions has functioned to draw the convert into a peculiarly personal bond with the priest.[9] In one respect this assumption tends to prove out among the friends of priests. This is the statement that more of the converts (58%) than of the others (47%) report that their parish priest has visited their home several times, or often, during the past year. The stated purpose of the priest's visit was more often for them (34%) a social or friendly call than it was for the non-converts (27%).

TABLE 6—Comparative frequency of parish priests' visits to homes of converts and non-converts in past year.

	(1944) Non-converts	(272) Converts
Not at all	35%	25%
Only once	18	17
Several times	29	35
Often	18	23

While the convert seems to know his parish priest more intimately than does the non-convert, his circle of clerical friends is probably not so wide. We find that half of the converts

(52%), and a somewhat smaller proportion (44%) of the non-converts had not entertained a non-parish priest in their home. Interestingly enough, there appears to be no difference in the degree to which both groups are acquainted with the bishop of their diocese. One-third of both categories say that they have met and talked with their bishop.

The observation that the convert makes about the priest's parochial tasks does not differ from that of the non-convert. They both rate in the same order the three most time-consuming tasks of the priest: first, finance and administration; second, counselling people, and third, directing parish organizations. Parish priests themselves rank these tasks in different order: first, counselling; second, directing organizations, and third, finance and administration.

We have seen that the converts come in greater proportions from areas of the country in which the Catholic population is smaller. This is reflected also in the fact that more of them (53%) than of the non-converts (46%) say that the priest they know best is a pastor. We shall later test the suggestion that priests in small parishes in little towns are closer to their parishioners than the priests in big-city parishes.[10]

Given this combination of factors we may conclude that the closer personal relationship between the clergy and the converts is due not only to the fact of their conversion to Catholicism. This is unquestionably an important factor, but as in most examples of sociological analysis, multiple factors must be taken into consideration.

Estimation of Clergy

Does the convert have a higher appreciation of the parish priest's work than is the case with the non-convert? The assumption may be made in general that he has a higher regard for what the Church does and offers, that he values deeply the religion he has embraced, and that he esteems more highly than the non-convert the functions of the clergy.[11]

TABLE 7—Comparative appraisal by converts and non-converts of selected functions of parish priests.

	(1944) Non-converts	(272) Converts
Sermons "very well" prepared	35%	46%
Priest "very much" encourages vocations to seminary	36	43
Priest "completely" favorable to laity in liturgy	52	61

This hypothesis is persuasively demonstrated with a consistent margin on the questions that were used to test it. The convert, for example, is more likely (46%) than the non-convert (35%) to say that the sermons he has heard during the past year were very well prepared by the priest. He says also in greater proportion (43%) than the non-convert (36%) that the priest he knows tries "very much" to encourage boys to study for the priesthood. He is also more likely (61%) than the non-convert (52%) to say that his priest friends are completely favorable to the laity's participation in the liturgy.

There is, of course, the possibility that the priests who are best known by these convert parishioners are also objectively more active and zealous than most other parish priests.[12] We have no way of identifying these particular priests among the large numbers of priestly respondents to the present study. On each of the above items, however, the priests have a much lower estimation of themselves than the converts have of them.

TABLE 8—Comparative opinions of converts and non-converts on work demands made on priests and other professionals.

	(1944) Non-converts	(272) Converts
Priest must work harder	41%	47%
About the same	38	34
Not so hard	21	19

TABLE 9—Comparative opinions of converts and non-converts on the worries of priests and of married men.

	(1944) Non-converts	(272) Converts
Priest's are greater	44%	52%
About the same	28	26
Priest's are less	27	22

While the convert may have a more sympathetic view of the parish priest, the non-convert may have a more realistic interpretation of the priest's work and worry. More of the converts (47%) than of the non-converts (41%) believe that the parish priest has to work harder than other professional men, but only one-third of the priests themselves make this claim. The converts also feel in greater proportion (52%) than the non-converts (44%) that the priest's "worries" in general are greater than those of married men. Less than one-fifth (18%) of our priest respondents hold this opinion.

Opinions about facts tend to be interpreted as attitudes toward the persons connected with the facts. In the present study we have no way of empirically measuring and comparing the objective facts on how the parish priest works harder than other professional men, or how his worries are greater than those of married men. Thus, the interpretations that people make become important, and the assumption turns into fact that the converts have a higher estimation than the non-converts of the priest's daily work.

Appreciation of the Laity

One of the main activities of the parish priest is centered in the direction of groups of lay people, the "parish societies." It seems clear that the laity's position and functions vis-à-vis those of the pastor in a Protestant congregation are considerably different from the usual procedures in a Catholic parish. If there is any area of Church life in which previous Protestant experiences might linger among converts, it ought to be in the relative positions of the clergy and the laity.[13] The hypothesis we are testing, therefore, is the question whether the converts place greater faith in the laity than the non-converts do.

TABLE 10—Comparative opinions of converts and non-converts on the cooperation of adult laity in parish projects.

	(1944)	(272)
	Non-converts	*Converts*
Eager and enthusiastic	22%	15%
Fairly cooperative	58	63
Reluctantly cooperative	12	13
Mostly uncooperative	8	8

When we asked them to judge the spirit of cooperation of most of the adult parishioners when an important project is underway, we found little difference in the opinions of these two categories. Eight out of ten of the respondents feel that the people are cooperative in the parish, but the proportion of converts (15%) who find them "eager and enthusiastic" is somewhat lower than that of the non-converts (22%). In this regard, the non-converts match the opinion of the priest respondents to this study (21%).

TABLE 11—Distribution of respondents who say that lay officers and leaders have initiative and responsibility.

	Initiative	Responsibility
(145) Male converts	44%	85%
(127) Female converts	50	93
(1130) Male non-converts	48	84
(814) Female non-converts	59	88
(2183) Parish priests	39	78

If the converts have a fairly high estimation of the spirit of cooperation among their fellow parishioners, they have somewhat less regard for the qualities of leadership, as expressed in the initiative and responsibility of lay group leaders and officers. The male converts appear to be the most critical among the categories we have compared, except for the parish priests themselves. Males are more critical in both categories, and converts are more critical than non-converts.

It could be suggested that parishioners who are critical of the lay leaders would want the priest to have more control in the parish organizations. This reasoning is complicated by the contrasting expectations among converts: that they would prefer the lay people to manage their own groups, but that they are dissatisfied at the lack of competent leadership among the laity.

The great majority of parishioners, both converts and non-converts, seem to feel that the parish priest should have more than an equal vote with the laity. Most of them believe that he

TABLE 12—Comparative opinions of converts and non-converts on position priest should take in parish groups.

	Non-converts		Converts	
	(1130)	(814)	(145)	(127)
	Males	*Females*	*Males*	*Females*
Equal vote with laity	16%	16%	24%	12%
Advice and counsel only	55	61	55	57
Veto and final decision	24	20	19	28
Complete control	4	3	2	3

should be in a position to counsel and advise parish groups, even on matters that are not strictly religious and moral. This appears to be a recognition of the executive function of the priest in all affairs of the parish. The male converts, however, include a substantial minority (24%) who would restrict the priest to an equal vote with the parishioners.

The converts are not striving for a reversal of the roles of priest and parishioner. When we asked them what single most important change was needed in their parish, about one-tenth of both converts and non-converts would like the bishop to remove the present pastor. This does not mean that they are in favor of a wholesale shifting of pastoral personnel. Indeed, they seem to prefer stability of parochial appointments in general. More of the converts (54%) than of the non-converts (47%) feel that both pastors and curates should be given relatively stable and permanent appointments by the bishop.

In so far as we can draw a conclusion from these data, we may say that there appears to be some dissatisfaction among the converts, especially the males, with the way in which the laity operated in the parish. Here again, the statistical differences are not significant, but the converts are in general less likely than the non-converts to praise the spirit of cooperation among the laity or the qualities of initiative and responsibility among the lay leaders.

Summary

Whether or not the convert to Catholicism feels like a stranger long after he joins the Church probably depends as much on his fellow parishioners as it does upon himself. Seven out of ten of them come into the Church before the age of thirty years, when they are still flexible enough to make the adaptations that their new religion requires. Yet, most of them retain throughout their life certain distinguishing characteristics.

1. By the criteria of education, income, and occupation, converts are hardly distinguishable from the other friends of priests. The fact that they come from all levels of society is a reflection of the fact that the Church itself represents all social classes.

2. The parish priest seems to take a solicitous interest in his convert parishioners by visiting their homes with some regularity. The convert, however, does not have so wide a circle of clergy friends who are not parish priests.

3. Converts in general seem to have a higher esteem of the parish priest than does the "born" Catholic who is probably more likely to take his priests for granted. They appreciate the functions of the clergy and have more sympathy for the difficulties of parochial tasks.

4. Converts do not seem anxious to increase the authority of the laity or to decrease that of the parish priest. They are not significantly more critical of the laity than are their fellow parishioners who are not converts.

NOTES

1. As in other areas of the Sociology of Religion, more research has been done on conversion by Protestants than by Catholics. See the review of thirty-two studies by W. J. McKeefery, *A Critical Analysis of Quantitative Studies of Religious Awakening* (Unpublished thesis, Union Theological Seminary, 1949), also David Moberg, *The Church as a Social Institution,* ch. 16, "Religious Conversion and Revivalism," and Paul B. Maves, "Conversion: A Behavioral Category," *Review of Religious Research,* vol. 5, no. 1 (Fall, 1963).

2. The *Catholic Directory,* for the years indicated, provides the following statistics for converts, from which the rate per thousand is derived.

Year	Number	Rate per Thousand
1930	38,232	1.9
1940	73,255	3.4
1950	118,347	4.3
1960	145,687	3.5

3. See the humorous and insightful account by Lucile Hasley, *Reproachfully Yours* (New York: Sheed and Ward, 1949); also among many "convert books," see Gilbert L. Oddo, *These Came Home* (Milwaukee: Bruce, 1954).

4. See *Social Relations in the Urban Parish,* p. 28; also Schuyler, *Northern Parish,* p. 221, who distinguishes converts according to the length of time they have been in the Catholic Church. Data from the Chicago Inventory Study allow us to make the following comparisons between Catholic and Protestant converts and non-converts. The table indicates frequency of Church attendance.

	Catholics		Protestants	
	Non-converts	Converts	Non-converts	Converts
Once a week or more	89%	56%	51%	40%
Irregularly	6	25	34	32
Seldom or never	5	19	15	27
Totals	(493)	(52)	(590)	(219)

5. See Fichter, *Southern Parish*, p. 40, and the further findings in *Social Relations in the Urban Parish*, p. 76.
6. John L. Thomas, *The American Catholic Family*, p. 190, says that "it is possible that the non-Catholic party who has no serious religious convictions may undertake conversion without fully calculating the cost of perseverance."
7. While territorial parishes may differ considerably in the class composition of membership, this reflects a local and neighborhood population rather than a process of "status-seeking." Conversion to Catholicism probably seldom indicates either upward or downward social mobility.
8. Shifting from one denomination to another by either clergymen or church members is not treated as "conversion" among Protestants. "Much movement between denominations reflects social aspirations and achievements. As a person climbs the ladder of socioeconomic success, he is likely to revise his activities within the church or even to change his church membership. High prestige congregations are especially likely to receive social climbers of different denominational background." See David O. Moberg, *The Church as a Social Institution*, p. 255; also Leila C. Deasy, "An Index of Social Mobility," *Rural Sociology*, vol. 20 (June, 1955), pp. 149-151.
9. In the present study, conversion to Catholicism and joining the Church are synonymous. Both terms are employed differently among Protestants, for whom conversion does not necessarily require a series of instructions, and joining a Church does not always imply conversion. See Moberg, *op. cit.*, "Why do people join Churches?" pp. 401-405, and the six definitions of conversion, p. 422.

10. See the discussion on Small-Town Catholics, below, ch. 9.

11. See Anton T. Boisen, *Religion in Crisis and Custom* (New York: Harper Brothers, 1955).

12. This is true of individual priests in pastoral work, but some congregations of priests, like the Paulists, also specialize in "convert making."

13. The influence that the laity has on the Protestant clergy is seen in Jerome Davis, "A Study of Protestant Church Boards of Control," *American Journal of Sociology*, vol. 38 (November, 1952), pp. 418-431. In the local Protestant parish, however, the minister is important as executive and decision-maker. In the eight Lutheran Churches where Kloetzli asked the question: "Over the last five years, who has had the most to do with deciding the program of your congregation?" four out of ten (38.6%) said they did not know. But of those who did know, six out of ten (58%) said the pastor, three out of ten said the local congregation, and the remainder (12%) said the denominational leaders. See Walter Kloetzli, *The City Church—Death or Renewal* (Philadelphia: Muhlenberg Press, 1961), p. 210.

CHAPTER EIGHT

Liberal and Conservative Catholics

So much confusion has been engendered in the debate about liberalism and conservatism in American society that we often have difficulty in merely defining the terms. Norms differ widely in distinguishing the liberal from the conservative. In the present nation-wide study we have employed two simple criteria. Liberals are those who favor the expansion of foreign economic aid and who also say that the primary desirable American social goal is the securing of the basic rights of all citizens, regardless of race or creed.[1] Conservatives are those who want to reduce foreign economic aid and who do not rate the securing of basic citizen rights among the three most important social goals.[2]

People who are liberal in some respects are probably conservative in others, but social scientists never tire of attempting to establish the structure of the liberal and conservative personalities.[3] If the present norms—and their limitations—are accepted, and if there is a recognizable liberal posture, differing from that of the conservative, we ought to find different answers to the questions of this study. In other words, the hypothesis that we are testing here is that liberals are more

adaptive, progressive, and outgoing; that they have a more
optimistic view of life and people.

We are not testing here whether Catholics are more liberal
than non-Catholics, or whether the friends of priests differ
significantly in this regard from marginal and dormant Catholics who hardly ever go to Church. All of these parishioners
are a special kind of Catholic. The parish priests too are a
special category of Catholic, and we shall be able here to
make some clergy-lay comparisons.

The Liberal Laity

In order to isolate as much as possible the normative factor
of liberalism and conservatism, we have matched the two
categories by sex and age. This statistical refinement meant
the reduction of the numbers so that there are 216 liberals
and 216 conservatives, and half of each of these is male,
half female. More of the conservatives are married to Catholics.

TABLE 1—Comparative marital status of liberal and conservative
parishioners.

	(216)	(216)
	Liberal	Conservative
Never married	20%	13%
Married to Catholic	71	81
Married to non-Catholic	9	6

The factor of differential education, both kind and amount,
may be of some importance in the background and attitudes of
these respondents. More of the liberals (47%) than of the conservatives (24%) have finished college; but more of the con-

servatives (45%) than of the liberals (36%) went to a Catholic high school.

TABLE 2—Comparative amount of schooling of liberal and conservative parishioners.

	(216) Liberal	(216) Conservative
High school incomplete	8%	9%
High school graduate	31	43
Some college	17	24
College graduate	29	15
Post-graduate studies	15	9

It is probably true to say that the person who has more education is likely to be a liberal, that is, answers positively the two questions on foreign aid and the securing of basic rights.[4] Perhaps this depends more importantly on the type of education that a person experiences. Yet it is also true that people having the advantage of higher education tend to come from a higher economic status. The expectation that people with higher income will be conservative, even if they have more education, is not disappointed in the present study.[5] The difference, however, is not significant; one-fourth of the liberals, and three out of ten (29%) of the conservatives report higher than average income.

TABLE 3—Comparative Catholic high school attendance of liberal and conservative parishioners.

	(216) Liberal	(216) Conservative
High school incomplete	8%	9%
Catholic and non-Catholic	5	8
All Catholic high	31	37
All non-Catholic high	56	46

The Liberal Clergy

From the responses of diocesan parish priests who cooperated in this nation-wide survey, we have also constructed the
two categories of liberals and conservatives, using the same
criteria to arrive at these designations. The importance of
matching these two types of priests by age and years since
ordination is immediately apparent in the fact that priests who
are under thirty years of age are much more likely (53%) to
favor the expansion of foreign economic aid than are the
priests who are over sixty (28%).[6]

TABLE 4—Comparative parochial assignment of liberal and conservative parish priests.

	(206) Liberal	(206) Conservative
Pastor of parish	45%	37%
First curate	38	39
Second curate	14	17
Third and fourth	3	7

The importance of matching these catgories for the age
factor is seen also in the fact that the liberals include more
pastors (45%) than do the conservatives (37%), even though
pastors are commonly thought of as being more conservative
than the curates who assist them. In this total study of priests.
where age is not controlled, the pastors are much less likely
(33%) than are the curates (46%) to be in favor of expanding foreign economic aid. The suggestion may then be made
that it is not so much the responsibility of the pastorate,
as it is advancing age, that makes the parish priest conservative.

Since the formal years of education enjoyed by the diocesan

parish priest are fairly standardized, we cannot weigh the amount of education as a factor of liberalism or conservatism. One significant influence, however, seems to be the place where the priest made his major seminary studies.[7] Almost half of the conservatives (48%) and a much smaller percentage (35%) of the liberals attended the major seminary in their own diocese.

TABLE 5—Comparison of dioceses where liberal and conservative priests made their major seminary studies.

	(206) Liberal	(206) Conservative
Own diocese	35%	48%
Other American diocese	48	40
Foreign seminary	17	12

If we work the statistics for the whole study from another point of view, we may note the extent to which the place of major studies seems to have an influence on the liberal or conservative attitudes of the future priests. Using the same norms of definition, but without controlling for age, we find that all three types of seminaries produce the same percentage of liberals, but that the foreign seminary seems to produce a smaller proportion of conservatives.

TABLE 6—Distribution of liberal, moderate, and conservative priests, according to place of major seminary studies.

	(882) Own Diocese	(939) Other American Diocese	(362) Foreign Seminary
Liberals	13%	14%	13%
Moderates	75	76	79
Conservatives	12	10	8

The suggestion may be made—and this is highly tentative—that the experience of studying outside one's own diocese helps to broaden the perspective of the future parish priest, and thus pushes him in a liberal direction. The hypothesis may also be suggested that the priest who made his high school course in a minor seminary would tend in the conservative direction. The evidence, however, does not warrant this assumption. In fact, a larger proportion of the liberals (47%) than of the conservatives (39%) made all, or some, of their high school studies in a minor seminary.[8]

TABLE 7—Comparative types of high school attended by liberal and conservative parish priests.

	(206)	(206)
	Liberal	*Conservative*
All minor seminary	33%	28%
Part minor seminary	14	11
Catholic high school	36	47
Non-Catholic high school	17	14

There are probably no rich men among the diocesan parish clergy and none who are living in dire poverty. Since salaries are nominal, it is practically impossible to use income as a norm of economic status, which in turn may have an influence on the social attitudes of priests. Nevertheless, we did ask about the personal financial savings of these parish priests. Actually, the two categories of priests do not differ in this regard. About half of them do have some personal savings, one-fourth are approximately solvent, and the rest are in debt. The earlier economic status of their family of origin, however, does show that the liberals are more likely (45%) than the conservatives (36%) to have come from a family with below average income.[9]

Some of the characteristics of these respondents, both priests and lay people, could probably be foretold without benefit of a nation-wide survey. For example, the liberals are more than twice as likely as the conservatives to read *America, Commonweal,* and *Atlantic Monthly.* More of the liberals read the syndicated columnists, and they liked Walter Lippman, while the conservatives preferred George Sokolsky. The conservatives read *Life, Reader's Digest,* and the *Saturday Evening Post* more than do the liberals. It is probably to be expected also that for both clergy and laity more of the liberals than of the conservatives lean toward the Democratic political candidates.

TABLE 8—Comparison in political preference by liberal and conservative clergy and laity.

	(422)	(422)
	Liberal	*Conservative*
Leaning toward Democrats	57%	40%
Toward Republicans	13	25
Independent voters	29	32

The regional distribution of Catholic liberals and conservatives seems to be fairly similar to that of other Americans, but the distinction between clergy and laity indicates some differences. In the Middle Atlantic States (New York, New Jersey, Pennsylvania) both priests and people are conservative. In the east north central States (Ohio, Indiana, Illinois, Michigan, Wisconsin) both priests and people are liberal. In the west north central States (Minnesota, Iowa, Missouri, the Dakotas, Nebraska, Kansas) the priests are more liberal than the laity. In the Pacific States (Washington, Oregon, California) the laity are more liberal than the clergy.

Social Involvement

The American Catholic has always been a socially aware person, even when the great masses of Catholics in this country were recent immigrants.[10] This is obviously a generalization to which many exceptions can be taken, and the present comparison shows that it is scientifically dangerous to stereotype Catholics as though they were all of one social mind. The central point in the present hypothesis is that the liberal Catholic, both laity and clergy, is more interested in social issues and more involved in them, than is the conservative Catholic.

TABLE 9—Relative proportions of liberals and conservatives, clergy and laity, interested in selected issues.

	(422) Liberal	(422) Conservative
International affairs	92%	83%
Race relations	91	68
Labor relations	75	60

Even though it is one of the characteristics of American conservatives that they dislike the foreign aid program, they do not express so much interest in international affairs as do the liberals. Another criterion is the conservative attitude toward securing the basic civil rights of all American people, which obviously involves the problems of race and segregation. The difference here is even greater between the social interest of the liberal and that of the conservative. While the proportion of the respondents who are interested in management-labor problems is not so great as in the other problem areas, the liberals are consistently higher than the conservatives.

TABLE 10—Relative proportions of liberals and conservatives, clergy and laity, interested in selected activities.

	(422)	(422)
	Liberal	*Conservative*
Community organization	65%	55%
Music, art, theater	66	56
Sports events	48	44

There is no inherent reason why the citizen who takes an interest in community organization should be either liberal or conservative in his social thinking. Conservatives are said to be organizing in increasing numbers. The same remark may be made about both cultural and athletic activities. Nevertheless a consistent pattern seems to emerge from the data of the present study. Even when the differences are small they always tend in the direction of a greater social awareness on the part of liberal Catholics. Whether this indicates a difference in personality structure cannot be determined from this evidence, yet the consistency of the findings is persuasive.

Religion is often described as a conservative factor, and the people who have the greatest religious interest are reputed to be the most conservative people.[11] All of these respondents are religious persons, and we made no attempt to measure degrees of participation. But when we ask the question about interest in religious and theological issues, we find that even here the proportion of liberals (90%) is higher than that of conservatives (81%).

The data from this study clearly confirm the hypothesis

that liberal Catholics are more socially involved and interested than conservative Catholics. The evidence is cumulative and consistent.

Attitudes toward the Seminary

It is difficult to hypothesize the probable attitudes of people toward seminary training on the general basis of their liberal or conservative personality. If the liberal is assumed to be an active and positive promoter of "good" causes, and if the layman's image of the seminary is a "good" one, then we may expect that our liberal respondents take a favorable view to seminary training. The data suggest, for example, that the liberal Catholics want their priest friends to encourage more vocations to the seminary. Six out of ten of them, as compared to seven out of ten of the conservatives, say that the priests do encourage vocations "very much."

TABLE 11—Relative proportions of liberal and conservative clergy and laity who would send elementary school graduate immediately to seminary.

(216)	Liberal laity	40%
(216)	Conservative laity	32
(206)	Liberal clergy	58
(206)	Conservative clergy	49

In this total study, as may be expected, more of the priests than of the laity are in favor of sending a young boy into the minor seminary for his high school training. If priests generally are more conservative than the laity, this preference might be interpreted as part of their conservative outlook. Yet, on the basis of the normative definition we are using here, the opposite has happened. Both laity and clergy on the liberal side are more in favor of the minor seminary. The significant factor, therefore, seems to be not whether one is a priest or parishioner but whether one is a liberal or a conservative.

TABLE 12—Comparative proportions of liberal and conservative priests who were well trained for several priestly functions.

	(206) Liberal	(206) Conservative
Lead a holy life	75%	64%
Lead an intellectual life	60	53
Deal with people	33	24
Cope with practical problems	24	19

Perhaps more revealing than the opinion of either lay persons or clergy toward the minor seminary is the way in which the priest appraises his own major seminary training.[12] In looking at the various functions for which the seminary prepares men, the liberal priests give a consistently higher estimation than do the conservatives. The majority of both categories say they were very well prepared to lead a holy and intellectual life; a minority of both say the same about their preparation to deal with people and to cope with practical parish problems. Yet, on all four items the liberal priests are consistently higher in their appreciation.

What these data show us is that the liberal Catholic in general has a more positive and favorable attitude toward seminary training, when their opinions are compared to those of conservatives. It is probable that the bishop and the diocesan officials get more support and encouragement from the liberal than from the conservative priests in their drive to increase vocations.

Laity Opinion of Priest Functions

The data of this study allow us to suggest that the liberal Catholic laity takes a less critical attitude toward the clergy than does the conservative. This does not mean that one is closer to objective reality than the other. For example, more of the liberals (48%) than of the conservatives (37%) believe that the sermons they have heard during the past year were "very well" prepared, but only about one-seventh of both liberal and conservative priests are willing to say that their own sermons are very well prepared.

More of the liberal laity (86%) than of the conservative (74%) say that the parish priests they know have a favorable attitude toward the participation of the laity in the liturgy of the Church. In this instance the clergy responses follow a similar pattern. The liberal priests are much more likely (68%) than the conservative priests (50%) to say that their clergy contemporaries fully approve lay participation in the liturgy. As a matter of fact, this stand on the laity in the liturgy is frequently used as a measure of the progressive priest.

TABLE 13—Comparative opinion of liberal and conservative laity on work load of parish priest and other professionals.

	(216)	(216)
	Liberal	*Conservative*
Priest works harder	46%	39%
About the same	39	34
Less hard	15	27

The liberal laity is more likely to say that the work burden of the parish priest is heavier than that of the other professional men. The liberal and conservative clergy do not show this difference of opinion on this question; and only three out of ten of both agree that they work harder than other professionals.

TABLE 14—Distribution of liberal and conservative opinion on comparison of priest's and married man's worries.

	(216)	(216)
	Liberal	*Conservative*
Priest's are heavier	48%	35%
About the same	32	28
Priest's are lighter	19	36

On the question whether the parish priest has greater worries than the ordinary married man, we find that the laity tend to be more sympathetic to the priest than the priest is to himself. Only 15 percent of both liberal and conservative priests believe that their worries are greater than the married man's. As in the question of professional burdens, the liberal laity are again more apt than the conservative to say that the parish priest worries more than the married man. In both of these questions the liberal or conservative posture of the clergyman does not seem to influence the answer, whereas the two categories of lay persons demonstrate distinctive answers.

The data of this study clearly affirm the hypothesis that liberal lay people take a more favorable and sympathetic attitude toward the work of the priest. They are more positive about the sermons they hear and about the priest's attitude on the liturgical movement. They also think that the priest

works harder and has more worries than the conservatives
are willing to admit.

Summary

The norms we have selected to distinguish liberal from conservative are logical in the sense that they constitute two of the
areas, foreign relations and civil liberties, on which liberals
and conservatives largely disagree. The data confirm this definition by consistently pointing up the positive and progressive
attitudes of the liberal category, both priests and lay people.
The general implication is that most of the attitudes of people
are colored by their liberal or conservative posture. Some of
the generalizations may be summarized here.

1. The liberal laity has had more years of schooling, and
more of them had attended public high school. Although the
two categories were matched for age and sex, the liberals
contained more who are single and more who are married to
non-Catholics. More of the liberal priests are pastors, more
attended the minor seminary high school and made the major
seminary studies outside their own diocese.

2. While American Catholics generally seem to favor the
Democratic Party in national politics, the liberals, both the
laity and clergy, lean much more heavily toward the Democratic candidates than do the conservatives. They tend also to
read the kind of periodicals that are called liberal. While the
data are not conclusive they indicate that the liberal Catholic
comes from a somewhat lower economic background than
do the conservatives.

3. The evidence of this study is consistent and conclusive
to the effect that liberals, both laity and clergy, are much more
interested in social problems. Their interest is greater also in

religious and cultural matters, and extends even to community groups and sports events. They are clearly more socially alert in all respects than are conservatives.[13]

4. The liberals take a more positive view of seminary training, even in the controversial question whether a boy who has just finished elementary school should enroll in the minor seminary high school. The liberal priests seem to be much more appreciative of their own seminary training. More of them than of the conservative clergy say that they were well trained in the major seminary.

5. The liberal laity takes a more sympathetic view of the functions of the parish priest. More of them than of the conservative laity say that the priest works harder than other professional men and that the priest has greater worries than the ordinary married man. More of them also think that the sermons they have heard were well prepared and that the priests they know are in favor of lay participation in the liturgy.

NOTES

1. This rough rule of thumb is mentioned also by Lenski, *The Religious Factor,* p. 188. "Liberals are those who favor equal rights for all, regardless of race or ethnicity," and a liberal is also one who "favors shouldering international responsibilities, participating in agencies of international cooperation such as the United Nations, and granting foreign aid to other nations."

2. The distinction we are making here obviously has nothing to do with the controversy between theological modernism and fundamentalism which for such a long time obfuscated the issues between science and religion. For modern usage and understanding of the terms, see Donald J. Thorman, *The Emerging Layman,* ch.

15 "Conservatives, Liberals, and Catholicism," Robert Cross, *The Emergence of Liberal Catholicism in America* (Cambridge: Harvard University Press, 1958), and the remarks of Daniel Callahan, *The Mind of the Catholic Layman,* pp. 94-96, 157-160.

3. These are not necessarily polar types. S. Stansfeld Sargent and Robert C. Williamson, *Social Psychology* (New York: Ronald Press, 1958), p. 509, place the reactionary on the other side of conservatism, and the radical on the other side of liberalism.

4. See the discussion above, ch. 2, on the least and the best educated among the friends of priests.

5. See the similar conclusions in Ernest Havemann and Patricia West, *They Went to College* (New York: Harcourt, Brace, 1952).

6. We have already discussed age differences above, ch. 6.

7. Even as late as 1962, the *Catholic Directory* reported that eighteen of the forty-eight States had no seminary, and sixty-nine of the 138 Catholic dioceses had no seminary, either major or minor.

8. For the influence of Catholic high school attendance on these friends of priests, see above, ch. 3.

9. "Liberals are generally identified with the working class and the intellectuals, and conservatives with the upper and middle classes." Although his data generally bear this out, Lenski, *The Religious Factor,* pp. 187 ff., warns against its overemphasis in what he calls the "post-capitalist" American society.

10. See Aaron I. Abell, "The Catholic Factor in the Social Justice Movement," and Fichter, "The Americanization of Catholicism," in Thomas T. McAvoy, (ed.) *Roman Catholicism and the American Way of Life* (Notre Dame: University of Notre Dame Press, 1960).

11. Most of the studies that use this terminology define religious liberals as those who have given up most of the traditional beliefs held by religious conservatives. In this theological sense all of these parishioners are conservatives. See Michael Argyle, *Religious Behaviour* (Glencoe: Free Press, 1959), pp. 174-177. Lenski, *The Religious Factor,* p. 190, points out, however, that religious heterodoxy has little or no relationship to political liberalism; so does Samuel Lubell, *The Future of American Politics* (Garden City: Doubleday, 1956), p. 122.

12. The most useful research material along these lines has been collected and analyzed by James E. Dittes, "Research on Clergymen: Factors Influencing Decisions for Religious Service and Effectiveness in the Vocation," in the Research Supplement to *Religious Education,* vol. 57, no. 4 (July-August, 1962), edited by Stuart W. Cook, pp. 141-165.

13. See this from another point of view in Fichter, "Anti-Clericalism in the American Catholic Culture," *The Critic,* vol. 21, no. 4 (February-March, 1963), pp. 11-15.

CHAPTER NINE

Small-Town Catholics

Catholicism is popularly known as a big-city religion in the United States, and it is unquestionably true that the overwhelming majority of American Catholics continue to live in urban and suburban areas. Among American religious groups, perhaps only Unitarians and Jews are more "urbanized" than Catholics. Yet, Catholicism is not limited to the sprawling metropolis. The *Catholic Directory* lists numerous parishes in villages and hamlets all over the country. One-fifth (20.6%) of the laity who provided data for this study live in small parishes in little towns where there is only one priest. About the same proportion (18.4%) of our clergy respondents live in places with less than 2,500 population.[1] At the other extreme, almost one-fourth (23.3%) of the laity live in large-city parishes where there are four or more priests; and one-fourth (25.9%) of the parish priests live in cities of over 100,000 population.

There are many differences between urban and rural (and small-town) Catholics, but we cannot here take up the argument whether religion dies in the city and flourishes in the country.[2] A nation-wide study of Catholic young men shows that the city boy more often has the opportunity to attend a Catholic school, but the country boy has more contact with the parish priest. The Catholic in the small town is more faithful to religious practices, like Mass attendance and the reception of Communion, but the city Catholic is more likely to know his religious truths and prayers better.[3]

The purpose of this discussion is to test the hypothesis that small-town Catholics tend to have closer relations with the parish clergy, greater parochial solidarity, and a more intimate sense of community.[4] This hypothesis involves also the well-known sociological contrast between the primary, communal, *gemeinschaftlich* type of human relations, and the secondary, associational, *gesellschaftlich* type. It is a frequently assumed proposition throughout the literature of the sociology of religion that a high degree of social solidarity is an inherent function of the religious group.[5]

Small-Town Laity

Who are these small-town Catholics, friendly to the priests? It is obvious that most of them live in places away from the North Atlantic seaboard and also outside the large metropolitan areas.[6] While they live all over the United States, they are over-represented in the Great Plains States and on the Pacific Coast. They are not quite so well off financially, since they are twice as likely (13%) as the big-city dwellers (6%) to have below average income.

Only one out of ten of these small-town parishioners is single as compared to almost twice as large a proportion (19%) of the big-city Catholics.[7] Although the percentages are small, they are also somewhat more likely to be in mixed marriages; and this is undoubtedly explained by the sociolog-

TABLE 1—Comparative income according to place of residence.

	(457) Small-Town	(1242) Medium	(517) Big-City
Above average income	18%	30%	26%
Medium income	69	63	68
Below average	13	7	6

ical finding that the rate of mixed marriages is higher in the less-populous areas where Catholics are in the minority.[8] This religious disparity of the population probably also accounts for the fact that converts are more numerous (14%) in the small towns than in the large cities (9%).

TABLE 2—Comparative marital status of small-town and big-city friends of priests.

	(457) Small-Town	(1242) Medium	(517) Big-City
Never married	10%	15%	19%
Married Catholic	82	79	76
Married non-Catholic	8	6	5

Married persons:	(409) Small-Town	(1056) Medium	(419) Big-City
Married Catholic	88%	93%	94%
Married non-Catholic	12	7	6

Catholic educational facilities are also less available in the smaller places. Half of the small-town parishioners (52%), as compared to four out of ten (41%) of the big-city people, attended a full four years at a public high school. The small-towners were only half as likely (21%) as the big-city people (41%) to have had an all-Catholic high school education,[9] but the amount of schooling attained in these different places also varies considerably. Almost six out of ten of the people in the small towns (57%), as compared to four out of ten (42%) of the big-city Catholics, did not attend college.

TABLE 3—Comparative Catholic and public high school education of small-town and big-city parishioners.

	(457) *Small-Town*	(1242) *Medium*	(517) *Big-City*
No high school	10%	4%	3%
High school incomplete	11	8	10
Four years Catholic high	21	36	41
Four years non-Catholic	52	45	41
Mixed Catholic and public	6	7	5

TABLE 4—Comparative amount of schooling of small-town and big-city parishioners.

	(457) *Small-Town*	(1242) *Medium*	(517) *Big-City*
High school incomplete	21%	12%	13%
High school graduate	36	29	29
Some college	20	21	19
College graduate	23	38	39

The advantages of an academic family background are not significantly different between the small-town and the large-city parishioners. Most of these Catholics, nine out of ten in both categories, came from families in which neither father nor mother had attended college. Yet, the educational level that people attain is not merely a function of family background or of years of formal schooling. It may be indicated by the kind and amount of reading that they currently do. About seven out of ten of both categories say that they read for relaxation, and more than nine out of ten say that they are interested in reading for information.

Small-Town Clergy

The parish priests in the villages and rural areas differ considerably from their big-city confreres. They are somewhat older men, averaging 45.19 years, as compared to 39.28 years for the city priests. This means, of course, that they have been longer ordained and have had more experience in the priesthood. Three-quarters of them (76%), as compared to half of the big-city priests, have been ordained more than ten years. The most important status differential is in the fact that the great majority of small-town priests are pastors.

TABLE 5—Comparative parochial status of small-town and big-city priests.

	(401) Small-Town	(1486) Medium	(296) Big-City
Pastors	86.8%	36.4%	18.6%
Curates	13.2	63.5	81.4

Like the parishioners they serve, the small-town priests tend to be at a lower economic level than the big-city priests. This judgment is derived from a question about their financial savings, answered by the priests themselves. The statistical difference in this regard becomes more significant when we realize that the small-town priests are older and have thus had a longer period in which to accumulate personal financial savings.

Most of the small-town priests are in dioceses which did not have a minor seminary at the time they were attending high

TABLE 6—Comparative financial status of small-town and big-city parish priests.

	(401) Small-Town	(1486) Medium	(296) Big-City
Has some savings	51%	55%	61%
Approximately solvent	23	24	21
Broke or in debt	26	21	18

school. Although the bishop often sends boys of high school age to minor seminaries in other dioceses, this probably accounts for the fact that only one-fourth of them studied all four years of high school in a minor seminary.

TABLE 7—Comparative type of high school attended by small-town and big-city priests.

	(401) Small-Town	(1486) Medium	(296) Big-City
All minor seminary	25%	25%	37%
Part minor seminary	14	12	15
Catholic high school	44	43	32
Non-Catholic high school	17	20	16

Since all diocesan parish priests receive approximately the same amount of professional seminary training, in which they study philosophy for two years and theology for four years, it is difficult to make a comparative judgment about their higher education. Since fewer of the small-town priests attended the minor seminary, it may be expected that more of them (32%) than of the big-city priests (20%) attended college before starting to study for the priesthood. The majority of them did their major seminary studies outside their own dioceses.

TABLE 8—Location of major seminary in which small-town and big-city priests studied.

	(401) Small-Town	(1486) Medium	(296) Big-City
Own diocese	22%	38%	77%
Other American diocese	57	45	15
Foreign seminary	21	17	8

It is probably true that an urban resident finds it easier to keep up his academic activities and interests. Libraries and lectures are more available in the larger centers of population, and we find in this study that both clergy and laity in the big cities show more interest in music, art, and the theater than do the priests and people in the small towns. There is also a dissimiliarity in the amount and kind of periodical reading that these respondents do. Only the *Reader's Digest* and the *Saturday Evening Post* are read by a substantially higher proportion of small-town residents.

TABLE 9—Percentage in each category who read selected periodicals "often" or "sometimes."

	Small-Town Laity	Small-Town Clergy	Big-City Laity	Big-City Clergy
America	14%	51%	43%	60%
Commonweal	14	34	29	37
Life	85	73	90	77
Reader's Digest	91	76	88	69
Saturday Evening Post	80	60	80	52
Time	74	68	83	80
U. S. News & World Report	58	52	57	52

It is probably to be expected that the priests read *America* and *Commonweal* in greater proportions than the lay people do, and this difference may be attributed to both educational background and religious interests. But there is also a difference in readership of these two periodicals between the small-town and the big-city clergy, and this may be due to more than residential location. It is also notable that while *Commonweal* is edited and published by laymen, it seems to be read more by the clergy than by the laity.

Clergy-Lay Relations

Do the parishioners in small places have closer personal relations with their priests than the people in big cities? One of the general assumptions about small-town living is that there exists a much greater feeling of community and more personal contacts among people.[10] That this generalization may extend also to clergy-lay relations is indicated by the fact that more of the small-towners (38%) than of the city folk (31%) say that they have personally met the bishop of their diocese. More of them (36%) also than of the big-city people (23%) have seen the bishop when he visited their own parish.

TABLE 10—Extent to which the bishop takes personal interest in the parish priest.

	Small-Town	Medium	Big-City
Much or quite a bit	31%	24%	14%
More or less	37	32	23
Little or not at all	31	44	62

The priests themselves are conscious of the distance between themselves and their bishop, and the parishioners report the facts about their personal contact with the bishop. The small parishes exist mainly in the smaller dioceses where the bishop is able to visit and to have a more positive, personal relationship with the priest and the people. This is reflected also within the parish. The lay friends of the priests in small-town parishes have visits from their pastor much more frequently than occurs in the big-city parishes.[11]

TABLE 11—Comparative frequency of visit of parish priest to laity during preceding year.

	Small-Town	Medium	Big-City
Not at all	22%	35%	41%
Only once	14	19	18
Several times	40	27	28
Often	24	19	13

TABLE 12—Comparative purpose of parish priests' visits to homes of parishioners.

	Small-Town	Medium	Big-City
Friendly social call	34%	28%	23%
Parish affairs	29	25	24
Spritual or sick call	15	12	12
No visit	22	35	41

The small-town parishioner seems to be involved in both social and parochial relations with the clergy. The priest is much more likely to stop in for a friendly call and he is also somewhat more likely to come to the lay person's home on parochial business. The city Catholic sees the priest more often in the rectory office than he does in his own home, and this may be the reason why the city priest is somewhat more (31%) favorably disposed to have regular office hours than is the country priest (17%).

TABLE 13—Comparative distribution of priests and people in small-town and big-city parishes.[12]

	Small-Town	Medium	Big-City
Priests per parish	1.18	2.45	3.06
Laity per parish	659.6	3,361.5	4,734.2
Laity per priest	554.5	1,369.2	1,543.5

Quite aside from the friendly spirit that is said to prevail in small parishes in rural areas, the size of parishes in relation to the number of priests must be an important factor in personal contacts and home visits. The average big-city parish has seven times more communicants in it than the average small-town parish. The average big-city parish priest has almost three times as many people to take care of as has the average small-town priest. It is true, of course, that the city parish is more compact. Most people live within walking distance of the rectory, while in the small towns the priest probably has to use his auto in making most parish calls.

At any rate, the hypothesis that clergy-lay relations are closer in the small-town parish tests out affirmatively by these data. Both priest and people in the small town see the bishop more often in their own parish, and they meet each other more often in the homes of parishioners. The size of parishes and the number of parishioners involved in these relations probably constitute the main reasons for these differentials.[13]

Solidarity of Lay People

While the priest is the key person in every parish, the manner in which the lay people cooperate with him and with each other spells the ultimate social success of the parish itself. All of the lay respondents to this study are fairly friendly to the clergy and are generally reputed as active Catholics and good parishioners. Are the qualities of group cooperation found more in the small-town parish than in the big-city parish?

One index of a cooperative spirit is the interest people show in community organizations and groups. By their own testimony, more of the small-town (72%) than of the big-city (64%) parishioners are interested in and involved in community organizations. The proportions for the clergy are less, yet more of the small-town priests (50%) than of the big-city priests (44%) say that they have a continued or greater interest in civic organizations. One may expect from these data that group life is more vital in the small-town parish.

We asked both the priests and the laity to gauge the extent to which the parishioners cooperate when there is an important parish project under way. The interesting contrast here is that the laity in the city have a higher estimation of their spirit of cooperation than the priests do. In the small towns the opposite is true. Priests there think more highly of the laity than the laity does of itself.

TABLE 14—Comparative opinion of laity and clergy of parishioner cooperation in small town and big city.

	Small-Town		Big-City	
	(457)	(401)	(517)	(296)
	Laity	Clergy	Laity	Clergy
Above average	77%	82%	82%	78%
Average cooperation	16	12	12	10
Below average	7	6	6	12

While the spirit of cooperation seems to be fairly high in all of these parishes, regardless of their location, the estimate

TABLE 15—Comparative opinion of laity and clergy of initiative and responsibility of lay leaders in small-town and big-city parishes.

	Small-Town		*Big-City*	
	(457)	(401)	(517)	(296)
	Laity	*Clergy*	*Laity*	*Clergy*
Have initiative	48%	25%	57%	43%
Have responsibility	86	74	88	78

of leadership qualities differs considerably. Lay people everywhere have a higher opinion than the priests have of their lay leaders' abilities. The qualities of initiative and responsibility seem to be higher in the urban areas; yet three-quarters of the priests in both places also think that the lay leaders show responsibility in the performance of their group tasks.

The most significant difference among all these categories of opinions lies in the low proportion of small-town priests who recognize initiative in their lay leaders. Even though they give their parishioners the highest ranking for cooperation, they also give their lay parish leaders the lowest rating for initiative. We have seen that both the clergy and the laity in the small-town parish are more interested and involved in community organizations. The implication here seems to be that the small-town people require more leadership from their priests than is the case in the large city. One-fifth of the small-town priests, as compared to less than one-tenth (8%) of the big-city priests, say that their lay leaders demonstrate neither initiative nor responsibility in the performance of their role.

The tentative conclusion to this hypothesis is that the small-town parishioners have a greater feeling of social solidarity, but that they tend to be followers rather than leaders.[14] We have seen that they enjoy fewer years of schooling, less Catholic education, do less serious reading, and are of lower economic status. It is probable that all of these factors must be taken into consideration in the search for an explanation of this generalization.

Burdens of the Parish Priest

Are small-towners more sympathetic to the parish priest's role than city people are? Do the parishioners in each place see the role of the priest in about the same way that the priest sees it? Is the city priest busier than the rural priest? Since the priest in the small town usually (87% of the cases) has no curate to assist him, he probably has to perform a greater variety of functions. On the other hand, since his parish contains fewer souls he may not be quite so hard-pressed by the demands of the job.[15]

TABLE 16—Comparative ranking of the most time-consuming tasks of the small-town and big-city priest.

	Small Town		Big City	
	Laity	Clergy	Laity	Clergy
Finances	1	1	1	4
Liturgical functions	2	7	5	7
Counselling	3	4	2	2
Hearing confessions	4	3	7	3
Parochial school	5	2	4	5
Lay organizations	6	5	3	1
Sick calls	7	6	6	6
Preaching	8	8	8	8

Assuming that the priests know better than the laity what task actually consumes most of their time, we have here clear evidence of the difference of parochial burdens. The small-town priest is greatly involved in the financial problems of the parish and in the operation of the parochial school. The big-city priest is more involved in directing parish groups and in counselling than in anything else. Both kinds of priests agree that liturgical functions and preaching take the least of their time among the listed parish tasks.

The small-town laity are correct in their ranking of the tasks of financial administration and of preaching. They think, however, that liturgical functions take much more time than they do; and that running the parochial school takes much less time than it does. The big-city laity are correct in their ranking of the tasks of counselling, making sick calls, and preaching. They are most in error, however, in placing financial tasks high above its proper rank, and confessions much below its rank.

Up to this point we have not really answered the query whether the city priest is busier than the country priest. Most city priests seem to put in a great deal more time with the parochial lay groups; and this derives from the fact that the urban parishes are more fully organized than the rural parishes.[16] The city priests spend more time working with the married couples (20%) than do the small-town priests (13%). But more of the latter (44%) than of the city priests (31%) say that most of their time is taken up with school children.

It may be said in general that the lay people have more concern about the priest's burden of work than the priest has for himself. For example, in both small town and large city more of the laity than of the clergy think that priests work harder than other professional men. Yet, lay persons in both places are more likely than priests to say that the priest gets his work done easily and quickly. They are more than twice as willing

TABLE 17—Comparative opinions concerning various functions of the parish priest.

	Small Town		Big City	
	Laity	Clergy	Laity	Clergy
Priest works harder than other professionals	40%	22%	42%	33%
Priest should have office hours in rectory	41	17	51	31
Priest gets work done easily and quickly	37	17	31	16
Priest's worries are heavier than married men's	51	22	40	16

in both places to say that the worries of the priest are heavier than those of married men.

Satisfaction and Discontent

We have seen that there exists a mutually respectful relationship between the laity and the clergy in both the small towns and the large cities. The degree of respect and esteem differs on some points. Let us look now at the way in which the priests appraise their own status and functions. Actually, both types of priests evidence considerable satisfaction with their present residential location. If they had a choice of pastorate, two thirds (67%) of the small-town priests, and a little more than half (52%) of the big-city priests would prefer to stay where they are.

While most of the small-town clergy would prefer to have a parish in a place with less than 2,500 inhabitants, only three out of ten (29%) say that they now have one of the best parochial assignments in the diocese. This appraisal is the more remarkable because most of the small-town priests are pastors

TABLE 18—Comparative preference of pastorate, if choice were given by bishop.

	Small-Town	Medium	Big-City
Country parish	19%	9%	6%
Small town	48	36	18
Suburban	10	19	18
Inner city	21	32	52
No preference	2	4	6

TABLE 19—Comparative rating of present parish assignment.

	Small-Town	Medium	Big-City
One of the best	29%	51%	47%
Fairly good	38	32	28
Middling	20	11	18
Pretty poor	7	3	4
One of the worst	5	3	2

and most of the urban priests are curates, and it is a demonstrable fact that pastors tend to be more content with their assignment than curates are.[17] Diocesan priests usually estimate the "best parishes" on several norms: size of the parish, condition of the physical plant, number of priests assigned to it, and the neighborhood in which it is located.[18] The opinion of the small-town priest is unquestionably influenced by these norms, quite aside from the satisfaction he feels in his own present work.

Although hardly any of the small-town priests employ secretarial help, and more of them than of the big-city priests have a pre-arranged work schedule, they are much less likely (22%) than the big-city priests (34%) to say that their work load is greater than that of the priest who performs non-parochial functions. We have also seen that fewer of the small-

TABLE 20—Comparative responses of clergy on some aspects of parish priest's work.

	Small-Town	Medium	Big-City
Works harder than non-parish priest	22%	20%	34%
Has paid secretarial employee	2	26	35
Has a daily work schedule	35	38	28

TABLE 21—Comparative proportions of small-town and big-city priests who find time-consuming tasks also satisfying and trained-for.

401 Small-Town Priests Most time-consuming	Also Most Satisfying	Also Best Prepared For
1. Parish finances	2%	3%
2. Parochial school	30	39
3. Hearing confessions	49	34
All three tasks	22	22
296 Big-City Priests Most time-consuming		
1. Parish organizations	3%	14%
2. Counselling people	24	22
3. Hearing confessions	36	48
All three tasks	19	26

town clergy (22%) than of the big-city clergy (33%) believe that they work harder than other professional men.

The typical diocesan parish priest does what has to be done in the rectory, in the church, and among the lay people, regardless of whether he considers it the most important task, the most satisfying, or the task for which he had been best trained. As an ordained priest of God, he unquestionably esteems sacramental functions, preaching, the liturgy, and other spiritual and religious functions as the most important duties of his life. Thus, among the three most time-consuming tasks of both the small-town and the big-city priests, the most satisfying is the sacramental work of the confessional.

The exigencies of parish life, however, force the small-town priest to spend most time on parish finances, a task which he finds least satisfying and for which he is least prepared and trained.[19] The same lack of satisfaction and of training occurs among big-city priests who have to spend so much time in directing parish groups. When we combine the three most time-consuming tasks in both the small-town and the big-city parishes, we find that about eight out of ten priests are mainly spending their time on tasks which are not most satisfying to them and for which they are not best prepared.

The tentative conclusion to this hypothesis is that the small-town priest shows more contentment with his lot than might be expected in the American society where urban-ward mobility is a pronounced sociological phenomenon. Few of the small-town priests are yearning to get to the city, even though most of them are urban-born, and even if the bishop would allow them a choice of a pastorate.

Summary

The urban-rural differences that persist throughout the American society are reflected to some extent in the small-town and big-city parishes. In the small towns both the priests and the people are at a lower economic level and they are somewhat older than the city folk. The parishioners there are less educated and have had less Catholic schooling. Most of the priests did not attend a minor seminary high school and had to get their theological training outside the diocese.

The main hypothesis of this chapter—that small-town Catholics have a greater sense of social solidarity—is for the most part confirmed by the data. This, too, is a reflection of a sociological generalization about the American people. Some of the sub-hypotheses contributing to this generalization may be briefly summarized.

1. Big-city parishes are approximately seven times larger than small-town parishes, and although they have more priests, each priest is responsible for three times more parishioners than is the small-town priest. If for no other reason than size, the small-town priest visits more often in the homes of his parishioners, and both he and the laity have closer relations with the bishops.

2. Both priests and people in the small towns are more involved in community organizations. The cooperation of the laity is appreciated somewhat more by the small-town priest than by the big-city priest, but this same esteem is not extended to the lay leaders. The city parishes appear to have lay leaders with a deeper sense of responsibility and much greater initiative than is the case in the small town.

3. The small-towners have somewhat more sympathy with the burdens of the parish priest than have the big-city parishioners. Neither type of parishioner, however, has a realistic knowledge of the tasks that consume most of the priest's time. All are fairly in agreement, however, that preaching and sick calls take relatively little of the priest's time.

4. The clergy in the smaller places are more content with their parish assignment than are those in the large cities. If they had a choice of pastorate, most of them would pick a country, or small-town, parish. Our data provide a clear indica-

tion, however, that both types of priests spend the most time on tasks for which they are least prepared and in which they take least satisfaction—the big-city priests in directing lay groups and the small-town priest in parish financial problems.

NOTES

1. Perhaps it is a validation of the sampling method used in this study that these proportions are the same as the estimated (19.4%) rural Catholic population. It has been demonstrated elsewhere that rural Catholic families are not contributing their share of vocations to the Church. Fichter, *Religion as an Occupation,* "Rural-Urban Background," pp. 73-78.
2. Concern about the city church is the theme of books like that of Gibson Winter, *New Creation as Metropolis* (New York: Macmillan, 1963). On the other hand, Truman Douglass complains about the "anti-urban bias which has become almost a point of dogma in American Protestantism." See his "The Job the Protestants Shirk," *Harper's Magazine* (November, 1958), pp. 45-49. For a view on urban Catholicism, see Fichter, "Integrative Functions of Metropolitan Religion," *The Harvard Divinity Bulletin,* vol. 28, no. 3 (April, 1964), pp. 73-83.
3. These differences have recently been confirmed (1963) in an unpublished survey on the "Catholic Background" of 4,171 young men in training for the armed services, conducted by the Social Science Research Program of Loyola University of the South.
4. For a study of a small midwestern rural parish, see C. J. Nuesse, "Membership Trends in a Rural Catholic Parish," *Rural Sociology,* vol. 22 (June, 1957), pp. 123-130. For a more general analysis, see Emerson Hynes, "The Parish in the Rural Community," in C. J. Nuesse and Thomas Harte (eds.), *The Sociology of the Parish* (Milwaukee: Bruce, 1951).
5. See the reference on this thesis in Fichter, "Religion: Integrator of the Culture," *Thought,* vol. 33, no. 130 (Autumn, 1958), pp. 361-

382; also the discussion by J. Milton Yinger, *Religion, Society and the Individual* (New York: Macmillan, 1957), pp. 60-72.

6. This distribution of small places is recognized in the proportion of Catholic "missions" as compared to parishes. In 1964, the Mountain States actually contained more missions (799) than parishes (670), while the New England States had six times as many parishes (1,629) as missions (260).

7. A tendency toward earlier marriage and a larger proportion of married people are characteristics of American rural areas. See Harold Phelps and David Henderson, *Population in Its Human Aspects* (New York: Appleton-Century-Crofts, 1958), pp. 83-86.

8. This is only one of the "factors influencing the rate of mixed marriages," as discussed by John L. Thomas, *The American Catholic Family,* pp. 155-158.

9. The number of Catholic high schools in any area is not so important as their accessibility to the Catholic population. For example, in New York State there are 271 Catholic high schools, a a ratio of one for 63,407 Catholics; in Utah there are only five Catholic high schools, and this is a ratio of one for 196,600 Catholics. These statistics are from the 1964 *Catholic Directory.*

10. For sociological descriptions of small towns, see William C. Mather, "Littletown, The Story of an American Village," *Harper's Magazine,* vol. 170 (January, 1935), pp. 199-208; and T. Lynn Smith, "The Role of the Village in American Rural Society," *Rural Sociology,* vol. 7 (March, 1942), pp. 10-21. For a more recent study, see W. D. Weatherford and Earl D. Brewer, *Life and Religion in Southern Applachia* (New York: Friendship Press, 1962).

11. See the description above on mutual visits in chapter 1, "The Closest Friends."

12. This table is derived from the data of the present survey in which we asked the approximate size of the parish where the priest worked and where the people lived. It is not derived from any "official" ecclesiastical statistics.

13. There is nothing deterministic or inevitable about this conclusion. The fact that a big-city parish can have frequent, close clergy-lay contact is demonstrated in Conor Ward, *Priests and People* (Liverpool: Liverpool University Press, 1961), pp. 54-65.

14. For other aspects of this problem, see Robert Lee (ed.), *Cities and Churches* (Philadelphia: Westminster Press, 1962), ch. 6, "Dilemmas of Urban Church Organization;" also Leo Sweeney, "A Religious Society in a Secular World," *Homiletic and Pastoral Review,* vol. 44 (December, 1943), pp. 197-204.
15. See Fichter, *Social Relations in the Urban Parish,* ch. 10, "Social Roles of the Parish Priest."
16. See the excellent analysis by John D. Donovan, "The Social Structure of the Parish," in C. J. Nuesse and Thomas J. Harte (eds.) *The Sociology of the Parish,* pp. 75-99.
17. Satisfaction with one's parochial appointment is a function not only of the rural-urban differential, but also of the position of pastor and curate.

	Small-Town		Big-City	
	(348)	(53)	(55)	(241)
	Pastor	*Curate*	*Pastor*	*Curate*
One of the best	30%	26%	64%	44%
Fairly good	38	40	22	30
Middling	19	25	12	19
Pretty poor	8	4	2	4
One of the worst	5	4	0	3

18. The most important single criterion used by curates is the reputation of the pastor in relation to his assistants.
19. "Every seminary course in pastoral theology would do well to include at least the elements of bookkeeping and the imparting of such commercial information as to give the priest the essentials of business procedure." James A. Magner, *The Catholic Priest in the Modern World* (Milwaukee: Bruce, 1957), ch. 6, "The Priest and Finance," (p. 96).

CHAPTER TEN

Growth of Bureaucracy

Catholics in the United States have organized many kinds of groups to perform many kinds of functions. National, regional, diocesan, community, and parochial groups have been formed in the pursuit of personal and social benefits. Some of these are large, loose groupings like the National Catholic Education Association, and others are small local primary groups, like the sub-parochial units of the Christian Family Movement.

The friends of priests are involved in, and affected by, these different kinds of social relations in various parts of the country. All of them, however, are parishioners and members of a specified diocese. We have already looked at the manner in which the small-town parish differs from the big-city parish, and we may now investigate the sociological differences in small and large dioceses.[1] The basic ecclesiastical structure of Catholicism is a territorial arrangement of dioceses, each with a bishop or archbishop at its head, and numbering 140 in continental United States in 1964.

As the Catholic Church grows in various sections of the country, the individual diocese becomes larger, involves more officials, performs more functions, and becomes more fully organized.[2] The sociological assumption is that the larger an organization becomes the more likely is it to develop a bureaucratic structure. This implies that procedures are routinized, traditions take on a sacred character, relationships become more formalized, and the social distance from top to bottom is increased.[3]

The annual statistics of the *Catholic Directory* show clearly that there are enormous differences in the size of American dioceses, and they provide a regional comparison between those areas where the Catholic population is numerous and those where it is most sparse. For example, in the five largest dioceses, Catholics constitute 38 percent of the population, and there are 762 Catholics for each priest. In the five smallest dioceses Catholics are about 2 percent of the population and there are only 301 Catholics for each priest.

Size as a Norm

Is there any evidence that bureaucratic change is occurring in the Catholic Church in America?[4] Do the larger dioceses have any of the characteristics that usually accompany large-scale organizations, and are these characteristics absent, or less evident, in the smaller dioceses? In order to test this hypothesis, we are comparing the responses from both the parish priests and their lay friends in the twenty-four largest dioceses with those in the twenty-four smallest dioceses.

These smaller dioceses have an average of only 66 diocesan priests and 44 religious order priests. They average fifty-two parishes per diocese, with 1,643 Catholics per parish. The largest dioceses have about ten times more priests and people on the average and about five times as many parishes. They average 649 diocesan and 440 religious order priests, 253 parishes in each diocese, with 3,485 Catholics per parish.

TABLE 1—Distribution of priests and parishioners according to size of diocese.

	Clergy	Laity	All Persons	
24 Smallest dioceses	115	136	251	5.7%
84 Medium dioceses	1088	1102	2190	49.8
24 Largest dioceses	980	978	1958	44.5
132 Total dioceses	2183	2216	4399	100.0%

In the comparisons we are making here, we find that about one-fifth of the dioceses—the largest—contain close to half of the people who have cooperated in the survey. At the other end of the range, about one-fifth of the dioceses contain only about 6 percent (5.7%) of the respondents. This is a fairly accurate representation of the so-called "maldistribution" of the Catholic population, but the decennial population census of the United States government shows also a regional maldistribution of the total American population.

TABLE 2—Diocesan distribution of size of parish by number of priests assigned to parish.

	Smallest Dioceses	Medium	Largest Dioceses	All Dioceses
Pastor only	42%	33%	13%	25%
Two priests	31	32	23	28
Three priests	18	25	34	28
Four or more	9	10	30	19

Catholics who live in the smallest dioceses are three times (42%) as likely as those who live in the largest dioceses

(13%) to be members of a one-priest parish. At the immediate parochial level this means a difference in the number of priests with whom the lay Catholic comes into contact. Catholics in the largest dioceses are three times as likely (30%) as those in the smallest dioceses to live in parishes where there are four or more priests. It must be remembered that this study covers only parishes that are operated by diocesan priests. It is quite possible that parishes run by priests attached to religious orders would show a different distribution according to numbers of both priests and parishioners.

The point to be made by these statistical comparisons is quite clear. There are more priests and laity, more and larger parishes, and bigger cities in the largest Catholic dioceses than in the smallest dioceses. These facts may appear obvious without the benefit of statistical demonstration, yet a significant sociological datum is that each priest in the smallest dioceses is responsible for less than half as many parishioners (301) as is the case of the priest in the largest dioceses (762).

Relations with Bishop

The bishop in the smaller diocese has the opportunity to visit parishes and to talk with people more frequently than is the case in the larger dioceses. More than half (57%) of the parishioners in the small dioceses, as compared to less than one fourth (23%) of the others, say that they have personally met their bishop or are on friendly terms with him. One priest in a small diocese remarked that this "open door" policy of the bishop is not always to the advantage of the clergy since it invites complaints, as well as compliments, from the laity.

The bishop in the smaller diocese is able to know his priests better and to act towards them in a fatherly manner that is not

TABLE 3—Comparative degree to which the bishop takes a "positive and personal interest" in the parish priest.

	(115) Smallest	(980) Largest
Much, quite a bit	44%	17%
More or less	30	25
None, hardly at all	25	57

possible in a large diocese where there may be a thousand or more diocesan priests.[5] This is seen also in the matter of parish appointments in which the bishop rarely consults the priest beforehand. More of the priests in the smaller dioceses (27%) than in the larger (17%) report that they discussed their present assignment with the bishop before the appointment was made.

One of the characteristics of a large-scale organization is the efficiency of the bureaus and offices that stand between the top authority and the rank and file of membership.[6] An analogy here is the diocesan chancery office, the efficiency of which is judged above average by eight out of ten (79%) of the big-diocese priests and by a smaller proportion (64%) of the little-diocese priests. There are probably fewer trained men to carry on the chancery job, the work does not seem quite so important, and there is a greater demand for priests in the pastoral functions of the smaller dioceses.

The Local Community

Since Catholics are less numerous in the communities of the smallest dioceses, the influence of both clergy and laity on the local community tends to be disproportionate. The implication seems to be that the individual cannot depend so much upon the prestige of the large organization, the Church, but upon his own individual activities as representative of the Church. This is most aptly demonstrated by the fact that one-third of the priests, as compared to one-fifth (21%) in the large dioceses, are active in civic organizations.[7]

The Catholic priest in the small dioceses does not have much opportunity to associate with other priests. The distance is often great between parishes, although automobiles and roads have tended to lessen the isolation from his fellow clergymen. Only about one out of seven (14%) of these priests, as compared to more than half (54%) of the priests in the large dioceses, has regular "outside" help from another priest for the Sunday Masses. Furthermore, a larger proportion (52%) of them than of the large-diocese priests (39%) also have religious tasks that are non-parochial. These are all diocesan parish priests, but in the metropolitan areas much of the non-parochial work, like chaplaincies, convents, and hospitals, is done by religious order priests.[8]

We have seen that the priest in the smaller dioceses has on the average a smaller number of parishioners in his spiritual care. He is therefore in a position to perform some of the non-parochial functions that have become specialized in larger dioceses, like teaching and youth work. He is also able to participate in civic activities outside the parish limits, like membership in the Elks Club, Library Board, and even the local fire department.

The laity from these small dioceses also report that the priests have more time in informal and friendly relations. They are twice as likely (44%) as the large-diocese Catholics (22%) to say that their parish priest drops in on them for a chat or a social call. It appears that the small-diocese priest goes to the people instead of waiting for the people to come to him. He visits more of his parishioners (57%) in their homes during the year than is the case with the large-diocese priest (42%). This is probably also the reason why he is more opposed (72%) to having regular office hours in the rectory than is the large-diocese priest (58%).[9]

In reference to the general hypothesis of this chapter, our data reveal here that human relations in the small diocese are not bureaucratized. Priests and people associate more frequently and informally, on a more personal and less official basis. In this situation the Church is more likely to be appraised because of the behavior of its clergy and members rather than because of the image of overwhelming strength that a large-scale organization presents to non-Catholics.

Kinds of Parish Priests

The highly structured large dioceses have efficiently organized their system of recruiting and training the clergy. Some of them, like Boston and New York, have been so successful in training priests that they are able to send them to other dioceses and to foreign missions. The Chicago archdiocese actually has more seminarians than it has diocesan priests. The average number of diocesan priests in these larger dioceses is 649, and the average number of seminarians being trained is 426, most of them in their own diocese.

The problem of recruiting priests and seminarians in the smaller dioceses is a serious one. Only four out of these twenty-four dioceses now have their own seminary, and these have been fairly recently established. As a consequence, the background of the priests in the small dioceses differs considerably from that of priests in the large dioceses. They are more than twice as likely (19%) as the others (7%) to have been born in a foreign country. Members of religious orders, who for various reasons resign from their organization, find the bishops of small dioceses receptive to their application. In fact, almost one-fifth (18%) of the priests in the small dioceses, as compared to 5 percent in the large dioceses, had formerly been members of religious orders. Most of them joined their present diocese while they were still seminarians.

Men who have a "delayed" vocation are more likely to find acceptance from the bishop of the small diocese who is in need of priests. In answer to a question about previous experience, almost one-third (32%) of the small diocese priests, as compared to a much smaller proportion (15%) of the others, said that they had begun in another occupation or profession before deciding to study for the priesthood. They had mainly had business experience, but some had also studied for a medical or engineering career.

There is no available comparative statistical information concerning the proportion of diocesan priests, or seminarians, who switch from one diocese to another. In the less populated, and less Catholic, regions of the country, like the Southern and the Mountain States, it is a fairly common experience to meet priests who were born and raised in the East and in the North. Whatever the amount of such mobility, it is mainly in the direction of the smaller dioceses.[10]

TABLE 4—Comparative age at which parish priests began studies in the seminary.

	(115) Smallest	(980) Largest
13-14 years old	23%	32%
15-17	23	21
18-20	29	28
21 years and older	25	19

The meaning of these comparisons concerning the background of priests ought to be evident. The priests in the smaller dioceses are not so thoroughly institutionalized in the patterns of their own diocese. They are more likely to have been "foreign-born," whether in a foreign country or in another part of the United States. More of them began in another occupation, and began their seminary training at an older age. Since few of these smaller dioceses have their own seminary, almost nine out of ten (88%) of these priests, as compared to three out of ten (32%) of the priests in the larger dioceses, made their major seminary studies outside their own diocese.

Satisfaction and Contentment

One of the paradoxes emerging from this study is the fact that priests who have studied outside their own diocese express more satisfaction with their seminary training than do the priests who attended the major seminary in their own diocese.[11] This appears to be particularly significant in the present context of small and large dioceses because of other personal satisfactions that are involved.

All categories of priests have a higher regard for the semi-

TABLE 5—Proportions expressing satisfaction with seminary training according to place of major seminary studies.

	(882)	(939)	(362)
		Other	
	Own	*American*	*Foreign*
	Diocese	*Diocese*	*Seminary*
Lead a holy life	69%	76%	79%
Lead intellectual life	57	62	71
Deal with people	24	35	39
Cope with practical problems	16	28	34

nary training they received in preparation for a holy and intellectual life than they have for the more practical kind of
preparation to deal with parishioners in the midst of parochial
problems. This differential is peculiar to all major seminaries,
whether domestic or foreign. The question of more importance
here is why the larger dioceses, which maintain their own
major seminaries, cannot elicit a higher rating of approval
from the men they train. There is, of course, a kind of normal
expectation of loyalty to one's own organization—in this case,
the seminary and the diocese to which one belongs.

TABLE 6—Comparative proportions of parish priests in smallest
and largest dioceses expressing satisfaction with seminary training.

	(115) Smallest	(980) Largest
Lead a holy life	78%	71%
Lead intellectual life	70	59
Deal with people	37	30
Cope with practical problems	30	22

When a man looks back at the seminary he attended, the
estimate he makes involves two aspects: his own subjective
personality and the objective reality of the major seminary he
is appraising. In the present comparison we have seen that the
priests from the smaller dioceses differ on several counts. They
were older and had wider experience before starting the seminary and not so many of them are natives of the diocese in
which they now work.

Seminary experience may look different because the man
who is looking at it is different. The other aspect of this appraisal is the objective competence of the major seminary itself

TABLE 7—Types of high school attended by parish priests from
smallest and largest dioceses

	(115) Smallest	(980) Largest
All minor seminary	23%	32%
Part minor seminary	16	13
Catholic high school	36	40
Non-Catholic high	25	15

as it is operated in the largest dioceses. We can merely speculate
on the sociological principle of bigness as a factor of bureaucratization. The seminaries in the largest dioceses average
226 students from the diocese itself and 30 from other dioceses.
This would not be a large student body in any regular college
but would be fairly large for the ordinary professional school
of a university.

It may be assumed that the policies of the seminary reflect
those of the diocese. The men are preparing for work in an
organization where traditions and procedures have become
institutionalized, where relations tend to be impersonal and
official. This is probably why the most frequently made suggestions for the improvement of the major seminary centered
around the human treatment of the seminarians.[12] Our respondents stressed most often the improvement of faculty-
student relations, the lessening of regimentation, the treatment
of students "like adults."

Career Characteristics

In most kinds of occupations the person who is interested
in career mobility and promotion tends to drift to the more
populous areas of the country where opportunities and pros-

pects are brighter. From the point of view of organization size, however, the ambitious person asks himself whether the large or the small organization has more room at the top, has many intervening steps on the ladder of promotion, follows a system of quick promotion of talented personnel.[13]

These considerations are, of course, merely analogous when applied to the priestly vocation in the Catholic diocese.[14] By the nature of his calling the diocesan priest is not ambitious for higher prestige and status, but he is also destined to only one major promotion, that of the pastorate.

TABLE 8—Comparison of average number of years to become pastor in smallest and largest dioceses.

	(24) Smallest	(24) Largest
5 years or less	9	0
6-10 years	14	0
11-15 years	1	1
16-20 years	0	13
21 years or more	0	10

In the smallest dioceses the newly ordained priest is practically assured of becoming a pastor within ten years, and the average length of time is 6.7 years. In the largest dioceses the priest has to wait three times longer, the average length of time being 21.9 years. Of course, the numbers of parishes and of parishioners are much greater in the larger dioceses, but the proportion of diocesan priests to the number of pastorates is also greater. In the smallest dioceses the priest is almost sure to be appointed to a pastorate before he reaches the age of thirty-five, but in the largest dioceses the priest may be fifty years of age and still be a curate. In some of these places the newly ordained priest is now being told that he may never be a pastor.[15]

The responses to this study show that two-thirds of the priests in the smallest dioceses are pastors, as compared to three out of ten (31%) in the largest. When we ask the parishioners about the priest they know best, we find that seven out of ten (68%) of these priests are pastors in the smallest dioceses, while four out of ten (41%) of the priests in the largest dioceses have a pastorate. This means, of course, that there are many more curates among the diocesan priests in the largest dioceses, and that the priest in the smallest diocese is twice as likely to be a pastor.

Not only is promotion to the pastorate more rapid in the smaller places, but the priest's estimate concerning the basis for promotion seems to be quite different. Generally speaking, in the Catholic diocese the bishop chooses new pastors accord- ing to the seniority list by year of ordination. This is why cu- rates in large dioceses can pinpoint exactly the number of years it takes to become a pastor by checking the ordination class that is now being appointed. This seems also to be the reason why priests in the largest dioceses are almost three times as likely (51%) as those in the smallest (18%) to say that the main basis of promotion is seniority. On the other hand, pastors —who are more numerous in the small dioceses—like to think that promotion comes mainly through merit and achievement.[16]

Aside from the question of achievement and seniority as the basis of promotion, a significant difference shows up here concerning preferment by the bishop, which appears to be a more prevalent occurrence in the smaller dioceses. Preferment can mean not only the appointment of a man before his turn occurs, or before he has proven himself, but also the appoint- ment of a priest to a "better" parish. All of the curates in the

TABLE 9—Comparative opinion of priests in smallest and largest dioceses on main basis for promotion to pastorate.

	(115) Smallest	(980) Largest
Mainly achievement	52%	37%
Mainly seniority	18	51
Preferment by Ordinary	24	11
No opinion	6	1

diocese are in fairly close agreement in the rating of the "better" and the "worse" parishes.[17] What seems to be implied here is that the appointment to a pastorate is more routine in the largest dioceses and more personal in the smallest dioceses.

We have seen that the bishop is closer to his priests and takes a more personal interest in them in the smallest dioceses. This may have a negative connotation in the sense that the priest here is under more narrow scrutiny, has less freedom of action, and can thus be judged more sharply and accurately by his superior, the bishop. On the other hand, the priest in the large diocese may feel that he is "just a number" in the chancery files, that the bishop would not know his name if he met him on the street, and that this relative anonymity frees him from too close scrutiny.[18]

These reflections return us to the general characteristics of bureaucracy in large-scale organizations. The fulfillment of routines and regulations tends to be the standard by which the functionary is judged. Where bureaucracy is less evident, in the small-scale diocese, a priest is more likely to be judged on his performance. The opportunity is greater for the parish priest to become known personally to his superior as a dedicated, zealous and successful worker. By this means, he may indeed "earn" preferment from the Ordinary in the appointment to a pastorate.

Summary

Since the bureaucratic evolvement of the diocesan structure affects the functionaries, or priests, more than the parishioners, this discussion has focused on the clergy rather than on the friends of priests. The changes that have occurred are best tested by a comparison of the largest and the smallest dioceses, because it is large-scale organization of every kind that necessarily demands a bureaucratic arrangement of programs, personnel, and procedures.

1. Church bureaucracy is furthest developed in America in those places where the Catholic population is most numerous and the ratio of priests to laity is lowest. In the smaller parishes in smaller dioceses personal contact between priests and people is more frequent.

2. The bishop in the smaller diocese has a more immediate concern about his parish priests and tends also to meet more frequently with the parishioners. This seems to mean that he handles more of the diocesan business personally and without the aid of numerous chancery intermediaries.

3. Parish priests and their lay friends appear to meet more frequently in the relaxed atmosphere of the home than in the prearranged setting of the rectory office. The majority of all priests are opposed to regular office hours, but this opposition is much stronger in the smaller dioceses.

4. Certain background characteristics, while in the minority, are found more in the priests in little dioceses: foreign birth, delayed vocations, former members of religious orders. They

are working in dioceses where relatively few local boys go to the seminary.

5. More of the parish priests in the small dioceses seem to be satisfied with their seminary training, and also seem to be fairly content with the parochial assignment that they now have. It is probable that studying at a major seminary outside their own diocese helped them to escape the formalization and impersonalization that occurs in larger dioceses.

6. The opportunity for fairly quick promotion to a pastorate, the career objective of most diocesan priests, is probably one of the most attractive aspects of the priest's commitment to a small diocese. Zeal and ability are more easily recognized and more quickly rewarded where the "competitors" are not so numerous.

NOTES

1. The focus was more on the parishioners themselves in ch. 9, above, on "Small-Town Catholics."
2. See this concept in another context in Fichter, *Religion as an Occupation*, ch. 9, "Organized Social Relations."
3. "We may take increased size of organizations, proliferation of authority levels, development of systematic organization rules, standardization of tasks, emphasis upon impersonal obligations, and separation of personal from official affairs as evidence of increasing bureaucratization." Robert C. Stone, "The Sociology of Bureaucracy and Professions," pp. 491-506, in Joseph S. Roucek, *Readings in Contemporary American Sociology* (Paterson: Littlefield, Adams, 1961).
4. It seems necessary to point out that bureaucracy is not always a pejorative term even though it is used often as a source of "tensions" between Catholics and Protestants. See, for example, Paul Horton and Gerald Leslie, *The Sociology of Social Problems* (New

York: Appleton-Century-Crofts, 1960), ch. 8, "Religious Problems and Conflicts."

5. The New York Archdiocese had ten auxiliary bishops in 1962. All of the larger dioceses have auxiliary bishops, but in the present study the bishop refers only to the Ordinary of the diocese, that is, to the bishop or archbishop who had episcopal jurisdiction.

6. The contrast is clearly demonstrated when one compares a diocese like Crookston, Minnesota, which requires only two pages in the 1962 *Catholic Directory,* and has only one vicar general and one chancellor, with an archdiocese like New York, which takes up twenty-seven pages, and has two vicar generals, three chancellors, two vice chancellors, and five assistant chancellors.

7. The big-city priest is more wary of "involvement" with non-Church groups. One of them said, "a lot of these people want you at their gatherings as a kind of endorsement, and a priest has to be careful that he doesn't seem to favor one group over another."

8. In the United States, 39% of all priests are in religious orders or congregations. But this percentage rises in the smaller, "missionary" dioceses, like Hawaii where it is 88%, Georgia 66%, and Corpus Christi, Texas, 62%.

9. The routinization of procedures, symbolized by regular office hours, and the specialization of functions, as indicated by less extra-parochial work and contact, in the larger dioceses, are characteristics of the bureaucratic system. See the discussion by Robert Dubin, *The World of Work* (Englewood Cliffs: Prentice-Hall, 1958), p. 364.

10. This means also mainly in the direction from urban to rural and small town. It is generally assumed that the opposite migration occurs among Protestant ministers, but this assumption was questioned by Ralph A. Felton, *New Ministers* (Madison: Drew Theological Seminary, 1949), pp. 25-26.

11. See how this factor of seminary locale relates to the attitudes of parish priests, above, ch. 8, "Liberal and Conservative Parishioners."

12. "Since functionaries minimize personal relations and resort to categorization, the peculiarities of individual cases are often ignored. But the client who, quite understandably, is convinced of

the 'special features' of his own problem often objects to such categorical treatment. Stereotyped behavior is not adapted to the exigencies of individual problems." Robert Merton, "Bureaucratic Structure and Personality," *Social Forces,* vol. 18, no. 4 (May, 1940), pp. 560-568.

13. For pertinent examples from a variety of occupations and professions, see the contributions to Sigmund Nosow and William Form, (eds.), *Man, Work and Society* (New York: Basic Books, 1962), ch. 9, "Career Patterns."

14. This problem is discussed in wider perspective and in more detail in Fichter, *Religion as an Occupation,* pp. 165-180. It is discussed also in relation to ministers and rabbis in W. Seward Salisbury, *Religion in American Culture* (Homewood: Dorsey Press, 1964), ch. 10, "The Clergy," and in David Moberg, *The Church as a Social Institution* (Englewood Cliffs: Prentice-Hall, 1962), pp. 501-505.

15. In the group discussions we held with priests in the larger dioceses, a persistent suggestion was that parishes should be smaller. The explanation was that this not only opens more opportunities for pastorates, but mainly allows more efficient administration of the priest's work.

16. Among all the parish priests who responded to this survey the pastors and curates differ in their opinion concerning the basis for promotion to the pastorate as follows:

	(944) *Pastors*	(1239) *Curates*
Mainly achievement	47%	33%
Mainly seniority	27	54
Preferment by Ordinary	23	12
Other (or no) opinion	3	1

17. The high rating of a "good job" among diocesan curates depends mainly on the personality of the pastor of the parish. Among the pastors the main criterion is the bigness of the parish (requiring several curates) and the physical facilities of the parish plant.

18. In group discussions with the clergy we found that the older priests would like their bishop to be the considerate "fatherly type," while the younger priests, especially in the larger dioceses, think there ought to be some kind of personnel manager for them in the Chancery office.

CHAPTER ELEVEN

The Image of the Parish Priest

Through the eyes of their friends among the laity we have looked at the diocesan parish priests of America, and have found many differences and contrasts in both the priests and their parishioners. The friends of priests are old and young, conservative and liberal, living in small towns and big cities—and so are the priests. The parishioners are single and married, poorly and well-educated, converts and born Catholics, upperclass and lower-class. They are active and cooperative parishioners, and like people everywhere they have their likes and dislikes.

We have seen then what kinds of friends the priests have. Let us now attempt a composite image of the priest who is their friend and spiritual father. If we may use here the analogy of the professional man and his client, we may ask whether the self-conception of the parish priest corresponds to the image that his clients, or parishioners, have of him.[1] To the extent that this occurs the priest is probably more effective and successful in his parish work.

Social scientists speak much about "role expectations," and the assumption is that people know what to expect when they go to a lawyer, hire an architect, or deal with a teacher. As an occupation becomes better known, and as its functions become more clearly delineated, there is a greater likelihood of agreement of expectations between the professional and his client. The relationship is smoother and the function is performed more expertly.

What do parishioners expect from their priests? What do parish priests understand by the role they are performing, and to what extent do they fulfill this role? A traditional textbook answer does not satisfy these queries, at least, not for any given time in any given culture. We asked American diocesan parish priests to tell about themselves, and we asked their best parishioners to tell about their priests. Since the priest is trained for his job, and is working at it, he is also the one who best perceives what his role is and ought to be. Since these adult parishioners are the best friends of priests, they are competent to express their opinions on the basis of day-to-day observation and experience.[2]

The parish priest is a man of many functional roles and for this reason he presents multiple facets to the parishioners he serves. Except for the casual and uninitiated observer, the priest cannot be described by the single pastoral image of the shepherd taking care of his flock. We must, therefore, analyze a series of images, and build them up on a comparison of both clergy and lay opinions. This is not a typology of different kinds of priests, but it is a way of looking at the parish priest in the performance of his different roles. The priest is seen then as (a) executive, (b) insolvent businessman, (c) overburdened professional, (d) spiritual leader, and (e) personal friend.

Image I: The Executive

The concept of the multiple role is a commonplace in all occupational analysis, but it appears to be particularly applicable to the parish clergyman. The pastor is the responsible supervisor of the parish unit, and he is supposed to be "all things to all people," which means in practice that he must do many things for which he was not trained in the seminary.

TABLE 1—Comparative ranking by priest and parishioners of the priest's most time-consuming task.

	Priests	Parishioners
Counselling people	1	2
Directing organizations	2	3
Financial administration	3	1
Parochial school	4	6
Hearing confessions	5	5
Attending the sick	6	8
Convert instructions	7	7
Preaching	8	9
Liturgical functions	9	4

What does the parish priest do with his time? To what extent do priests and parishioners see the same thing in the same way? When we asked the parishioners what they consider the most time-consuming task of the priest, they put in first place the job of financial administration, in second place, counselling people, and in third place, the direction of parish organizations.[3] The priests agree that these three tasks take most of their time, but they put counselling in first place, running organizations in second, and the financial role in third place. They say that liturgical functions take the least amount of time, while the parishioners rank this in fourth place.

In any comparative judgments of this kind it is obvious that the priest has the facts in the case, and that the judgment of the parishioners represents a somewhat distorted image of the main functions of the priest. We did not ask them what the

TABLE 2—Comparative ranking by priests of their own most time-consuming, most satisfying, and best trained-for work.

	Time-Consuming	Most Satisfying	Best Trained-For
Counselling people	1	2	3
Directing organizations	2	8	8
Financial administration	3	9	9
Parochial school	4	7	7
Hearing confessions	5	1	1
Attending the sick	6	3	5
Convert instructions	7	4	4
Preaching	8	5	6
Liturgical functions	9	6	2

priest does best, or what they consider the most important functions he performs.[4] We did, however, ask the priests themselves what they found most satisfying in the work they do, and what tasks they do, and what tasks they were best trained for.

It is likely that every seminarian looks forward to celebrating Mass, administering the sacrament of penance, and giving spiritual counsel to people, and these are the tasks for which the parish priests say they were best trained in the seminary.[5] Yet, in actually serving the people in his parish, the priest is obviously performing the functions that have to be done. It is a curious fact that three of these activities, for which he feels least competent, and in which he gets the least personal satisfaction, are among those that use up most of his time. These are parochial functions that can probably be performed well by other than an ordained minister of God.[6] Laymen can certainly handle financial management; they do in many places operate schools; and they are probably competent to direct their own parochial organizations.

One of the critical questions we asked the parishioners indicates their willingness to assume at least some of these parochial responsibilities. When we asked them what single change they would like to make in order to improve their parish, the most frequently mentioned suggestions were to involve the laity more in the parish and to bring the laity closer to the clergy.[7]

These findings imply a two-fold distortion of the parish priest's pastoral image. In the first place, the parishioners see the priest spending a great deal of time on tasks that are essentially non-sacramental. Except for counselling, he is largely serving his people in tasks that are subsidiary to his priesthood. It is no wonder then that the parishioners have a central image of the priest as the organizer or executive of an enterprise. This is an image too that the priest by instinct and training would like to repudiate.

A more serious distortion is that which exists between the training and interests of the clergy on the one hand, and the tasks that they must perform on the other. They rate executive and financial activities as those for which they are least prepared in the seminary, and which are most distasteful for them. Yet, these essentially secular tasks consume an excessive amount of time and energy.

Image II: Insolvent Businessman

Since the pastor is ultimately responsible to the bishop for the physical maintenance of the parish, he can hardly escape at least some aspects of the businessman's role. The fiscal responsibility and control of the American Catholic parish is in the hands of the pastor, who is obliged to make annual reports directly to the bishop of the diocese. Unlike the Catholic parish in some other countries, the American parish allows no authority, and encourages relatively little responsibility, among the laity for the material maintenance of the parish.

Although a financial statement is released once a year for the information of the laity, most parishioners seem to know very little about either the income or expenditure of their parish.[8] In one Northwestern parish we asked the people to estimate how much it costs to operate their parish for one week, and the range of guesses was from $300 to $3,000, with the average estimate at about $1,200. In spite of this variation, only 16 percent thought that the parochial income was less than the expenditure.

By American standards of managerial achievement this means that the ordinary parish priest is considered a successful entrepreneur. The friends of priests seem to be sophisticated enough to realize that when the priest "talks money" from the pulpit, he is not asking anything for himself but is pleading for the support of the parish (and for the wider needs of the diocese and Church.) Nevertheless, they are largely ignorant of the financial status of both their priest and their parish. They hear the yearly financial report, but have usually had no opportunity to participate in either the allotment or disbursement of the parish funds. This is probably why a clarification and improvement of parish financing is suggested by large numbers of the laity as the most needed change in their parish.

The parishioner's lack of knowledge about the priest's personal financial status seems to be even greater. Perhaps most people do not distinguish between the professional and the personal life of the priest, and give little thought to the fact that diocesan priests receive a salary and must support themselves. Their board and lodging—and sometimes the maintenance of their automobile—are provided from the parish funds, but they must otherwise take care of their personal needs from a relatively inadequate salary.[9]

It is not unusual that the pastor who is in charge of a million-dollar plant is himself a relatively poor man. Since he may actually reside in a well-appointed home or in a sub-standard house—depending on what the parish can afford—the priest's material standard of living, as well as his personal financial status, may be difficult of estimation by the parishioners. About one-fifth (22%) of the lay respondents think that their own standard of living is higher than that of the priest; and about the same proportion (23%) think that it is lower. The majority of the laity (60%), however, believe that their own financial worries are heavier than those of the priest they know best. Less than one-fifth (18%) feel that their own worries are lighter.

TABLE 3—Opinions of laity compared with factual statement by clergy concerning priest's personal financial status.

	(2183) Priests	(2216) Parishioners
Priest has some savings	55%	40%
Is approximately solvent	23	46
Is in debt	22	12

Can we say that the laity has an image of the priest as a successful business man who is personally poor? The great majority (94%) of these diocesan parish priests do have an automobile as their own personal possession. Half of them (51%) have a television set; almost a third (32%) own a collection of classical records; and more than a third (37%) own a high fidelity recorder. Some of these items are probably gifts from friends and relatives; but some of them which they have bought themselves are definitely not yet paid for. One-fifth (22%) of the priests report that they have personal debts.

The lay people underestimate both the debts and the savings of the parish priest. They are apparently unaware of both the potential sources of income and the financial obligations of the clergy. The diocesan priest often takes out insurance of various kinds, and must attempt to make some provision for his old age. Some of them, in the poorer dioceses, have not been away from their parish in more than five years because they cannot afford to take a vacation. A substantial minority (27%) are contributing regularly to the support of relatives, usually their mother. The younger priests in most dioceses are still paying off to the bishop the debt they contracted for their seminary education.

It is probably true to say that the parish priest, particularly the pastor, applies whatever fiscal competence he possesses to the financial problems of the parish. It is his task and re-sponsibility to collect and disburse the monies of the parish. The typical American pastor is relatively successful in this function, even though by the very nature of his priestly calling he may put no effort into the amassing of wealth for himself. The valid image of the average parish priest, therefore, is that of a successful entrepreneur who displays few of the personal and material marks of success. In this respect the lay people tend to have a confused image of the parish priest.

Image III: Overburdened Professional

The parish priest, especially in the urban areas of the United States, has a reputation among the laity as a busy and hard-working man. We have seen that there is some ambiguity, and some misinformation, concerning the kinds of tasks about which he is busy. Yet the lay people seem to think that the parish priest has efficient work habits. More than four out of ten (43%) of the priests say that they cannot keep up with their work, or are always far behind, but only 13 percent of the parishioners make this judgment about the priests they know.

TABLE 4—Comparative opinions of laity and clergy on whether priest's worries are greater than those of married men.

	(2183) Priests	(2216) Parishioners
Priest's are greater	18%	45%
About the same	19	28
Priest's are less	62	26

Worry often accompanies work, but it appears from our data that the parish priest worries much less than his lay friends think he does. The priest works for and worries about his whole flock, while a married man has a more constricted and personal concern about his wife and family. Even when we look separately at the married people's opinion, we find that a significant minority (43%) of them agree that the priest has a greater burden of worry than most married men have.

TABLE 5—Comparative opinions of laity and clergy on whether occupational demands are heavier on priest than on other professional men.

	(2183) Priests	(2216) Parishioners
Priest's are heavier	33%	42%
About the same	32	37
Priest's are lighter	35	21

From the point of view of work activities it is probably more meaningful to compare the occupational demands made on the parish priest with those made on other professional men. Here again, the friends of priests show great sympathy for the parish clergy. Eight out of ten (79%) of the lay persons, as compared to two-thirds (65%) of the clergy, say that the parish priest has to work as hard as, or harder than, other professional men.

TABLE 6—Comparative attitudes of laity and clergy on definite office hours for the parish priest.

	(2183)	(2216)
	Priests	*Parishioners*
In favor	25%	48%
Neutral	12	24
Opposed	63	28

If the accurate image of the parochial occupation is that which the priest himself entertains, it is evident that the priest works less hard, and has fewer worries, than the lay people realize. The functional ideal of the Catholic clergy is that the parish priest is always "on duty" and that he is ready to serve his parishioners at any time of the day or night. Yet, many of the laity seem desirous of making this availability more definite by the establishment of office hours in the parish rectory. The laity is twice as likely as the clergy to be in favor of this arrangement; but the priests are more opposed to it than the lay people are in favor of it. Actually, less than one-fourth (23%) of the parishes employ full-time secretarial help in the parish rectory.

This difference of opinion about the utility or advisability of regular office hours for the parish priest indicates that the laity generally has only a vague notion about what the priest does with his time. In one small-town parish that we studied eight out of ten (78%) of the parishioners have visited the rectory office during the past year, some of them many times. Parishioners do not come to the priest the way patients go to a dentist or a physician. They tend more to visit the rectory in their own free time, which is usually in the evening after dinner. This is also a time when the priest is occupied with parochial meetings and organizations. Because most of the day-time calls on the priest's time are irregular and unpredictable, only one-third of them report that they follow a regular daily work schedule. Many of the others say that a schedule of this kind is either unnecessary or impossible in parish work.

The American parish priest is unquestionably an activist when compared with the priests of some other countries. Yet, the parishioner's view interprets him as more busy and active than he really is. In so far as the image of the priest as an overburdened professional is a distorted one, its origin seems to lie in the time element surrounding his work. He is most busy, and has most contact with the parishioners, on weekends and evenings, the very time when his friends, the lay people, are free of their own occupational burdens.

Image IV: Spiritual Leader

We have seen that priests look upon themselves more as counsellors than as administrators, but that their lay friends have the reverse image of these tasks. The parochial functions for which they were best trained in the seminary are the type that are necessary for spiritual leadership. Above all, the priests rate highest the seminary training they have had which intended to prepare them to lead a holy life.

The spiritual leader must also be a preacher to his people, and while preaching is not considered a serious time-consuming task by either priest or parishioner, it is a more satisfying function for the priest than some of the other activities in which he must engage. Do the parishioners look upon their priests as good preachers? How closely does the priest's self-appraisal correspond to that of his lay friends? We did not ask them to evaluate the quality of the sermons, but only to estimate whether they were well-prepared.[10]

TABLE 7—Comparative statements of laity and clergy concerning sermon preparation.

	(2183) Priests	(2216) Parishioners
Well prepared	53%	81%
More or less prepared	15	14
Poorly prepared	32	5

The friends of priests are most generous in their high opinion of sermon preparation. The priests are not as well satisfied with their pulpit endeavors as the people are, and the high estimation of the laity may come as a surprise to priests who sometimes hear that there is much complaining in the pews. Another index of spiritual leadership may be found in the attitudes of priests toward the participation of the laity in the liturgy of the Church. We asked priests about their confreres, and parishioners about the attitudes of the parish priest they know best.

Only 8 percent of the lay people say that the priest they know best takes hardly any interest at all in promoting vocations to the priesthood; while more than one-third (36%) of the priests make this negative statement about the fellow clergy-

TABLE 8—Comparative opinions of laity and clergy on the attitude of parish priests to lay participation in the liturgy.

	(2183) Priests	(2216) Parishioners
In favor	58%	81%
Neutral	35	15
Opposed	6	3

TABLE 9—Comparative opinions of laity and clergy on extent to which parish priests encourage boys to enter seminary.

	(2183) Priests	(2216) Parishioners
Much, quite a bit	42%	66%
More or less	22	24
Hardly, not at all	36	8

men they know. From a positive point of view, two-thirds of the laity see their priest friends as more than ordinarily active in the recruitment of future seminarians; but only four out of ten (42%) of the clergy see this degree of active recruiting among their fellow priests.

The laity feels that the lack of priestly vocations is the greatest single problem facing the Church in America today; while the priests themselves believe that moral indifferentism and the religious school question are greater problems. We find then that the lay people seem to have more concern about the vocation problem, and believe that the priests are trying harder than they really are to solve this problem by getting boys into the seminary. On the other hand, in the practical matter of actually sending a thirteen-year old boy to the minor seminary, the priests are more ready (53%) than the laity (39%) to do this. Perhaps this means that the majority of the lay people would prefer to have the future priest make his high school studies outside the minor seminary.[11]

It is quite probable that priests set their expectations higher than do the lay people. They seem to think that their sermons should be better, and that priests in general should give more encouragement to the participation of the laity in the liturgical movement. A similar interpretation may be made of the extent to which parish priests encourage school boys to enter the seminary and study for the priesthood.

In these few examples of spiritual leadership, the general prestige in which the clergy are held is probably a factor in the layman's image of them. One may suggest further that clerical modesty about their own achievements tends to balance out this factor of prestige. Since both types of respondents are presumed to be objective and conscientious observers, the realistic image of the priest as a spiritual leader may be said to lie between the two variant appraisals.

Image V: Personal Friend

Since the lay respondents to this study were recommended by the priests as active collaborators in Church work, we may expect that there exist cordial relations between them and the clergy. Friendship is a matter of degree, and we have already discussed the difference between the closest and the more distant friends among the lay people. Seven out of ten of the lay persons say that their best priest friend usually has a happy and cheerful disposition. The overwhelming majority (85%) of the priests feel that cooperative relations among the diocesan clergymen themselves are happy and friendly. Yet only three out of ten (31%) of the priests say that their seminary training helped them very much, or quite a bit, to learn how to deal with people.

It is generally assumed that there is little anti-clericalism in the United States, either inside or outside the Church, and practically none of our respondents, priest or lay, rates this among the major problems facing the Church in America.[12] All of our data from this select category of parishioners show that the people who know the priests best are the people who have the highest regard for the clergy. Yet they would like to improve this relationship. When asked what single change they would suggest to improve their own parish, they mentioned most frequently a closer working partnership with the parish priests.

TABLE 10—Purpose of parish priest's visit to the homes of parishioners.

	(2216)
	Parishioners
Friendly or social call	28%
Parish business	25
Spiritual ministration	13
No visit (or no answer)	34

In the ordinary personal relations among people it is expected that friends visit one another's home. In the relationship between priest and parishioner in the United States, however, it appears that the parishioner visits the rectory much more than the priest visits the parishioner's home. The priest tends more often to make a social or friendly call to the parishioner, while the latter calls at the rectory more often on parish business or for spiritual counsel.

These are the friends of priests, and two-thirds of them say that their parish priest has been in their home at least once during the past year. More than half (55%) of these people had visits also from other priests, who are not from their parish. We must assume, however, that most of the modal and marginal parishioners—who are not contained in this study—seldom had a visit from a priest.[13] Taking the census, which was done within the last three years in two-thirds of these homes, is a functional kind of contact between parish priest and parishioners. There are, however, various techniques of census-taking which do not require the priest to visit every household in the parish.

The image of the parish priest as a friend of the people emerges quite clearly from these data, but the priest is not seen as one who mingles freely with the parishioners. The expected line of separation between the clergy and the laity is maintained in this regard. There is often a friendly or congenial purpose in the interchange of visits, but the combination of parochial affairs and spiritual ministration shows that the main reason for these visits is a functional one.[14]

Summary

In comparing the pastoral image as seen by the clergy and by the laity, the most significant finding is that the laity thinks more highly of the priests than the priests think of themselves. One may suggest that this is the professional modesty becoming to the man of God. One may suggest also, however, that the judgment of the laity reflects the genuinely high status that clergymen occupy in American society. Catholic lay people are by and large satisfied with their parish priest. They make use of his services, express high esteem for him, and are fairly cooperative when the need is manifest. Impatience and criticism by nuclear parishioners seem to be symptomatic of lay concern for potential improvement rather than of incipient anticlericalism.

Research in the sociology of occupations shows that professional rating—for efficiency and success—is done legitimately only by fellow professionals. The layman's appraisal is subject to this correction. The opinions expressed by priests concerning themselves and other parish priests must be accepted as more realistic and of greater validity. This fact does not derogate the importance of the image that the parishioners have of their priests. It is their appraisal, and it is a real one, that can immediately affect the priestly parochial role.[15]

1. The public image of the parish priest seems to be seriously distorted only in the functional roles he performs. Lay people tend to see him mainly as the administrator of an organized enterprise, who must worry about money problems, moderate lay groups, and concern himself about the elementary education of children.[16]

2. The ordinary criteria of successful management, symbolized by the income and style of life of executives in the commercial world, are not generally applicable to the diocesan parish priest. The contrast between the personal financial status of the priest and the flourishing condition of a large parish plant, is not fully appreciated in the layman's appraisal of the priest.

3. The American stereotype of the professional person does not allow him to be leisurely. Almost everybody says that "Father is always so busy!" The demands and worries of the job appear heavier to the parishioners than to the priest, but both clergy and lay people seem determined to disallow any public image of the "lazy priest." The best friends of the priest

continue to have an image of him as the overburdened professional.

4. The role of spiritual father, as counsellor and confessor, is the preferred self-conception that the parish priest entertains. Nevertheless, he continues to do what has to be done, even though his seminary training has not prepared him for it, and his personal preferences repudiate it. Even here, he is more modest about his sermons, the way he relates the liturgy to the laity, the extent to which he encourages seminary vocations.

5. The functional and organizational status of the parish priest requires that the analysis of friendship between the pastor and his people be modelled on the professional-client relationship. Intimate, relaxing, and friendly relations are more viable with non-parishioners, but even in this instance the sacred status of the priesthood precludes the normal friendship between equals.

6. The pivotal functions of the priest, and the conception that the laity has of them, are largely determined by the internal organization of the parochial system. The authority structure is relatively "flat." Responsibility and decision-making rest directly in the hands of the priest, while the laity remain in an ancillary position. This implies that the "new emergence" of the laity in the American Catholic Church will alter both the image of the priest and the organizational structure of the parish.

NOTES

1. This avoids, for the moment, the question whether the priest-parishioner relationship is similar to that of the professional to his client in which there is, ideally, little or no conflict of interest

between the two. See Ernest Greenwood, "Attributes of a Profession," in Sigmund Nosow and William H. Form (eds), *Man, Work and Society,* pp. 206-218.

2. Asking the parishioner's opinions about the priest does not presuppose here that he is a customer who is "always right" and who shops around till he finds what he wants. See Everett Hughes, "The Sociological Study of Work," *American Journal of Sociology,* vol. 57, no. 5 (March, 1952), pp. 423-425.

3. A study of eight Lutheran parishes by Walter Kloetzli, *The City Church—Death or Renewal* (Philadelphia: Muhlenberg, 1961), p. 206, found that the pastor's most time-consuming tasks, in the opinion of parishioners, were: preparing sermons, work for the Church at large, and attending Church meetings.

4. Schuyler's Northern parishioners, *op. cit.,* p. 175, estimated as the priest's most important role that of "preacher and teacher of God's word." Conor K. Ward, *Priests and People,* p. 147, found as the three most important duties: visiting parishioners, Mass and sacraments, sick calls.

5. We queried 348 diocesan minor seminarians and found that the priestly tasks they think they will "like most" are counselling and liturgical functions, and the ones they will "like least" are financing and preaching.

6. This is indicated also by one of the parish priests who remarked: "what justification do we have for receiving Holy Orders and then dedicating almost our whole life to these secular activities? Is this not our greatest waste of priestly talent and manpower?"

7. As one parishioner declared, "we want to leave the major decisions to the pastor, but we want to be heard, especially in the material, physical and financial problems of the parish."

8. In some places parishioners complain that the annual financial reports are too vague and generalized. "We foot the bills," said one layman, "we want the right to know how the money *was* spent, if not a voice in how it is going to be spent."

9. Lay people often find it hard to believe that in some dioceses a pastor's salary may be as low as one hundred dollars a month, and a curate's sixty dollars a month. It is difficult to strike an average

income for diocesan parish priests since the salary is fixed at different levels from one diocese to another.

10. Although Lutheran parishioners think their ministers spend much more time in sermon preparation, their appraisal of the preaching is fairly close to that of Catholic parishioners. About three-quarters (73.3%) like the sermons "very well" and one-fifth (21.6%) "fairly well." See Kloetzli, *op. cit.,* p. 208. See also the analysis of preaching in *Southern Parish,* ch. 16, "The Word of God."

11. It is also true that the majority of diocesan parish priests did not attend a minor seminary high school for four years. In fact, only about one-third (34%) entered the seminary at age fifteen years or younger.

12. See the discussion of this point above, ch. 4, "Social Class and Anti-clericalism."

13. We were able to test this in an unpublished nation-wide survey of 4,171 Catholic young men. In answer to the question, "Did the priest ever visit your home?" the proportions of those saying "never" were: Nuclears, 28%; Modals, 40%; Marginals, 57%; and Dormants, 69%.

14. The way in which patterns differ is shown by the experience of St. Catherine's parish in Liverpool. More than nine out of ten (94%) of the households are in regular contact with the priests, and 84 percent said that the priest had visited their home within the previous six weeks. Yet, this is considered "very little contact" by one parishioner who said, "the priest can call only once in six weeks now, and then only for ten or fifteen minutes. It was once a month but the parish has grown." Ward, *op. cit.,* p. 58.

15. The parishioners' expectations and conceptions probably do not influence the parish priest's functions to the same extent that they do those of the Protestant minister. See Luke M. Smith, "Laymen's Image of Parish Clergymen," *Proceedings* of the Society for the Scientific Study of Religion, (1958), p. 11. Another researcher concludes that the sharp distinctions Catholics make between the priest and the layman "are either in process of modification in the United States or have been modified where Protestants are in the majority." W. Widick Schroeder, "Lay Expectations of the Ministerial Role: An Exploration of Protestant-Catholic Differentials,"

Journal for the Scientific Study of Religion, vol. 2, no. 2 (Spring, 1963), pp. 217-227.

16. A small-town pastor has strong feelings on this point. "We waste too much time on youth activities. If we really want to do our work in the parish, we must sit down with parents in their kitchens."